Developing Resilience

Some individuals emerge from grim experiences stronger in mind and spirit than others who suffered the same fate. In this book, Michael Neenan suggests that it is the meanings that we attach to events, and not the events themselves, that determine our reactions to them. This is why different people can react to the same event in a variety of ways.

Developing Resilience shows how people can find constructive ways of dealing with their difficulties by using the techniques of cognitive behavioural therapy as well as listening to the wisdom of those who have prevailed over adversity. This book provides useful guidance and advice on topics including:

- managing negative emotions
- distinguishing between what is within and outside of your control
- learning from past experiences
- developing self-belief
- increasing your level of frustration tolerance
- maintaining a resilient outlook.

This book will be essential for anyone trying to find constructive ways forward in difficult times, as well as counsellors, coaches and therapists looking for guidance in helping their clients.

Michael Neenan is Associate Director of the Centre for Stress Management, Kent, an accredited cognitive behavioural therapist and author (with Windy Dryden) of *Life Coaching: A Cognitive-Behavioural Approach.*

Developing Resilience

A Cognitive-Behavioural Approach

Michael Neenan

Routledge
Taylor & Francis Group

LONDON AND NEW YORK

First published 2009 by Routledge
27 Church Road, Hove, East Sussex BN3 2FA

Simultaneously published in the USA and Canada
by Routledge
711 Third Avenue, New York NY 10017 (8th Floor)

Routledge is an imprint of the Taylor & Francis Group, an Informa business

Copyright © 2009 Michael Neenan

Typeset in Times by Garfield Morgan, Swansea, West Glamorgan
Printed and bound in Great Britain by TJ International Ltd, Padstow,
Cornwall
Cover design by Sandra Heath

British Library Cataloguing in Publication Data
A catalogue record for this book is available from the British Library

Library of Congress Cataloging-in-Publication Data

Neenan, Michael.
    Developing resilience : a cognitive-behavioural approach / Michael
Neenan.
        p. cm.
    Includes bibliographical references and index.
    ISBN 978-0-415-48068-0 (pbk.)
    1. Resilience (Personality trait) I. Title.
    BF698.35.R47N44 2009
    155.2'4—dc22

                                                              2009001495

ISBN: 978-0-415-48068-0 (pbk)

Contents

Illustrations

Preface

For as long as I can remember, I've been fascinated with individuals (e.g. prisoners of war, concentration camp inmates, those with severe disabilities) who not only survived great adversity but also emerged from their grim experiences stronger in mind and spirit. Why did they not see themselves as embittered victims whose lives would be forever blighted by these experiences as some others did who went through the same ordeals? What was their secret? In reading many biographies and autobiographies of these remarkable individuals, what stood out for me was their determination to prevail over their grim circumstances: to adapt to the new conditions they found themselves in and to find some constructive meaning to inform their struggles with adversity. Circumstances wouldn't dictate their responses, they would. In other words, they would choose what attitudes to adopt in these circumstances.

Similarly, as a cognitive behavioural therapist, I teach my clients that it's the meaning (attitudes) they attach to events, not the events themselves, which largely determines how they react to them: 'The key idea here is that, in general, people do not respond to *events* in their lives, but rather to their *interpretations* of events. The same event can lead to very different reactions from different people' (Antony and Swinson, 1998: 45; original italics). Pinpointing what your attitudes are is crucial to understanding how well or badly you're coping with adversity. In this book, discussions of resilience and the case examples used to illustrate it in action will be seen from a cognitive behavioural therapy perspective. The clients are composite characters in order to protect their identity and the dialogues I have with some of them are not verbatim but reconstructed for the sake of clarity – to emphasize certain points without the accompanying verbal clutter of rambling, humming and hawing, and going off at tangents.

Most of the problems my clients dealt with were largely within the realms of what you might expect to experience in your lifetime, nothing of the scale or grimness of the examples given above. This book is not intended to be a self-help manual with steps to follow and forms to fill out, but rather is offered as an appreciation of resilience: how adversity can be transformed into a personal triumph as demonstrated by the stories throughout the book of individuals facing and overcoming the various difficulties they were confronted with. I hope you will be able to draw some useful lessons from this book which will strengthen your own resolve to find a constructive way forward during tough times in your life.

I would like to thank my long-time colleague, Professor Windy Dryden of the University of London, who generously agreed not only to read the manuscript and suggest improvements to it but also contributed some valuable ideas to the development of the first chapter. Of course, any mistakes or shortcomings that are evident in the book are solely my responsibility.

Chapter 1

What is resilience?

Introduction

Imagine two people working for the same company at the same level and salary and both love their jobs. Unfortunately, they lose them when the company goes through a 'restructuring process'. They both experience initial bitterness and dejection ('Those bastards! After all the hard work and loyalty we've shown them. Might as well give up when you've been kicked in the teeth.'). But then they begin to show significant differences in dealing with this setback in the days and weeks ahead. The first person accepts, without liking it, that his job has gone and commits himself to finding another one. He welcomes support in this endeavour from his family and friends. Eventually, after several attempts, he secures a new job at a lower salary but is glad to be back in work and the chances of promotion are promising. How did he manage to keep on track during this difficult time? 'I don't know really. No point in staying miserable. That's not going to get me a job, is it? You've just got to get on with it, haven't you?'

The second person finds his initial bitterness strengthening and his drinking increasing as he broods on the unfairness of what has happened to him. His wife and children are reluctant to approach him as he snaps at them when they do. He is envious of his friends who have jobs and avoids their company. Attempts at finding a job are negligible. His wife, when she can summon up enough courage to approach him, suggests that he should talk things over with the GP. 'I don't need any help from her! I just want my old job back, then things will be all right again. Can't you see that?'

Why didn't both men react the same way (e.g. crack up or fight back)? After all, the event was the same for both of them. A starting point in attempting to understand resilience is to discover the meaning (attitudes) that people attach to adverse life events. The first man eventually concluded, 'No point in staying miserable. You've just got to get on with it', and looked for and found another job. The second man clung to the idea that 'I just want my old job back'. Mired in prolonged bitterness and helplessness, he avoided looking for a new job. People react differently to the same event based upon how they view it, which underscores the point that there is always more than one way of seeing events even if, at times, it is difficult to discern any other viewpoint than the current one (Butler and Hope, 2007). So being a flexible thinker (or attempting to develop such an outlook) rather than remaining locked into a fixed viewpoint allows for adaptation to challenging and changing circumstances.

The crucial importance of how our thinking powerfully influences our feelings and actions will be emphasized throughout this book. Examining our thinking provides an entry point into our inner world to discover whether our attitudes are helping, hindering or harming us in our struggle to deal with difficult times. Self-defeating and goal-blocking attitudes are targeted for challenge and change. Identifying, challenging and changing problematic thinking and behaviour is the basis of cognitive behavioural therapy (CBT) which I've practised for 20 years. The insights and techniques of CBT can help you to deal not only with your current problems (e.g. panic, depression) but also encourage you to develop a view of yourself as a strong and capable person who is able to overcome hard times, find happiness in life and pursue important goals – in other words, developing greater resilience.

Teasing out a person's attitudes may not reveal straightaway who is demonstrating resilient behaviour in times of misfortune: a snapshot of a particular moment in the struggle does not necessarily reflect who will make it in the longer term and who won't. Remember that both men were initially bitter and dejected when they lost their jobs because they both had the same view of the situation. If the snapshot had been taken at this point, could you really say which one would start to fight back and which one would give up? Additionally, showing hardiness in response to current adverse events doesn't mean you will always be hardy no matter what happens to you. Similarly, lapsing into despair for several months doesn't mean you will be stuck there forever. Meaning is not static and, therefore, is likely to change over time. Flash forward several years and the 'fighter' might be receiving psychiatric help following the end of his marriage ('I can't cope without her') while the 'giver up' may have his own moderately successful business ('I always wanted my own business, so why not give it a try?').

Resilience is an intriguing yet elusive concept: intriguing because it provides some kind of answer to why one person crumbles in the face of tough times while another gains strength from them, but elusive in that the concept resists a definitive definition. Some writers on resilience suggest 'that we will never completely understand it' (Coutu, 2003: 18). While I would not suggest there is anything mystical about resilience, no matter how many books I read on the subject, how often I talk to academics about it, and that I know what the factors associated with it are, it still remains something of a puzzle to me why one person can endure so much suffering and still remain largely optimistic and happy while another person, whose scale of suffering is much less, retreats into bitterness and victimhood.

Having said that, I will help you to increase your understanding of resilience, including examining some misconceptions about it, and show you how to develop greater resilience (most people already demonstrate resilience in some areas of their lives, past and present). The philosopher Tom Morris states that if you live long enough and pay attention to what is going on around you, 'you may come to understand one of the deepest truths about life: inner resilience is the secret to outer results in this world. Challenging times demand inner strength and a spirit that won't be defeated' (2004: 1). Resilience is the bedrock of positive mental health (Persaud, 2001).

Bouncing back or coming back from adversity?

The popular view of resilience is bouncing back from adversity, but I find it unhelpful in trying to understand better what resilience is. Bouncing back reminds me of a childhood toy I had: a blow-up, chest-high figure of Yogi Bear which, when punched, fell to the floor but sprang back immediately to the upright position. Bouncing back suggests a rapid and effortless recovery from adversity with barely a hair out of place, a poised and unruffled person, the envy of others who have to struggle, perhaps painfully and slowly, to overcome similar adversities. This might be the ideal that some wish to aspire to, yet it seems to be more of a comic-book view that may well trigger self-depreciation (seeing oneself as weak or inadequate) if this ideal is not realized in times of crisis. If the person can spring back so effortlessly, was it a genuine adversity she actually experienced? Is visiting your cantankerous and elderly parents for a weekend just as much of an adversity as being caught in a bomb blast?

Obviously adversity is determined subjectively. A situation that is viewed as an exciting challenge by one person such as public speaking ('It will give me a chance to shine') can fill another with fear because he believes he won't be able to control his nervousness and therefore will be laughed at. So a subjective view of adversity allows us to discover what a person's vulnerabilities are and what work might be needed to deal with them. As some adversities will be severe or extreme (e.g. being raped), work is likely to be slow and painful in these cases.

Some writers question whether labelling a situation as an adversity (e.g. a close friend moves away) automatically makes it one because you feel unhappy about what's happened (Grotberg, 2003). If you believe that the bad or disagreeable things that happen to you are all equally awful, then you have lost a sense of perspective, and developing resilience is likely to be stalled until this perspective is introduced, such as a 0–10 scale from disappointment to disaster. A resilient response to adversity engages the whole person, not just aspects of the person, in order to face, endure, overcome and possibly be transformed by the struggle (Grotberg, 2003) – coming back rather than bouncing back. As Walsh (2006: 3) observes: 'We must be careful not to equate competent functioning with resilience'. Taking in our stride the daily demands on our time and energy (e.g. by family, friends, work, unexpected and unwelcome events) is not the same coping process as attempting to deal with traumatic events like being kidnapped or losing a leg in a car crash.

Another point to consider with the 'bouncing back' from adversity image is this: Does your life return to exactly the same state it was in before the adversity? Imagine you have been injured in an accident and now suffer from chronic pain which is made barely tolerable only through medication. There is no quick and easy return to your pre-adversity state. In some respects it is gone forever while in other ways there are continuities in your life before and after the accident (e.g. still seeing some of the same friends, reading the same newspaper and watching the same television programmes). In my experience, clients usually, and understandably, get stuck in looking back to how it used to be before the accident – 'I just want my old life back' – before they reluctantly embark on the struggle to adapt constructively to the grim reality of their debilitated condition and search for some new and hopeful meaning in their lives. 'Bouncing back' suggests that little time would be allowed for this slow process of adaptation and discovery.

'Vulnerability is for losers'

Another unhelpful idea about resilience is that because you've been toughened by hard times you are now invulnerable – nothing can harm or crush you (how would you try to convince others, like a jury, that you have reached this superhuman level?). No matter how robust you've become by dealing with tough times, you still remain vulnerable to coping poorly with future adversities. Vulnerability is not a sign of weakness; no one has an absolute resistance to adversity. Resilience cannot be seen as a fixed attribute of the person – when circumstances change (e.g. being sent to prison, noisy neighbours moving in, prolonged ill health), resilience alters (Rutter, 1987). In these new circumstances, you might cope badly and believe that your resilient qualities have vanished as you assumed there would be an automatic transfer of them from one difficult situation to another.

For example, I was seeing a tough and highly capable manager who had been involved in a car accident and suffered cuts and bruises as well as shock; but the real shock for him was that he needed a week off work to recover. He had a normal human response to the accident but dismissed it contemptuously as 'being pathetic' and couldn't understand why he wasn't back at his desk the next day. He was bewildered by his actual response to the accident versus the ideal 'bouncing back' response he expected of himself. His fear was that he had lost control of himself, his toughness had deserted him. In discussing and accepting the ideas contained in the last paragraph, he reformulated his view of resilience in more realistic terms: 'Strong and capable, but still vulnerable at times. I need to remember that!' With this change in attitude, he took a more helpful, less condemnatory stance towards those of his colleagues he had previously dismissed as 'losers' when they complained of heavy workloads or missed performance targets.

What kind of strength?

Continuing the theme of strength through adversity, some books on resilience like to quote the nineteenth-century German philosopher Friedrich Nietzsche – 'Whatever doesn't kill me makes me stronger' – and assume it is self-explanatory. This is how resilience is forged, triumphing over tough times and making yourself tougher in the process (remember that whatever doesn't kill you can also leave you weaker or shattered by what you've been through). But they don't elaborate on the nature of the strength that has emerged: for example, has it made you more compassionate and helpful towards others' struggles or convinced you that there are only winners and losers in life and losers deserve what they get for their spinelessness and self-pity (as the manager above was previously inclined to believe)? If it is the latter view, you may have sacrificed or lost sight of your values (what's important to you) in the struggle to overcome hardship; resilience has turned into ruthlessness. As far as I'm aware, no writer on resilience advocates ruthlessness as part of a resilient outlook. The usual position is to stress the importance of 'being a compassionate and contributing member of society' (Brooks and Goldstein, 2003: 3) such as by teaching your resilience skills to others (if they are receptive) or doing charity work.

As I mentioned above, our values are often severely tested in times of crisis. If they appear to be lost in the struggle to do whatever it takes to keep your life on track (e.g. you've stopped your fitness programme as you believe it distracts you from the need to focus all your time and energy on trying to save your business from bankruptcy), remind yourself of what your values were when the crisis has abated, estimate how far you have strayed from them, and plan a course of action to get them back. Also, dealing with adversity brings into focus which values are more important (e.g. family, faith and genuine friendships) and which are less so (e.g. making lots of money, being seen with the 'right' people and working long hours). If it can be hard to keep your values when misfortune strikes, it can be equally difficult to keep them when success arrives. Self-discipline is abandoned, excess embraced and the benefits of success are squandered (e.g. all the money you won is gone because of your 'living for the moment' outlook and none of it invested to provide for your future needs). Being resilient applies to both good and bad times.

Resilience beyond reach?

Some self-help books on resilience (usually American) keep providing examples of individuals who have not only overcome adversity but also have then gone on to scale the heights of personal achievement in, for example, sports or business. While awe inspiring, these stories give the impression that resilience can only be achieved by an extraordinary few, not by the ordinary many. Therefore, in this book I want to move away from presenting a dazzling collection of resilience stories and focus on what I might call routine resilience: coping with the vicissitudes of daily life, tackling psychological problems and facing the inevitable adversities that lie in wait. Perhaps having the quiet satisfaction that you are stronger than you think is enough for most people without becoming paragons of resilience as well. The examples used, with some exceptions, are from my therapy practice.

Surviving, but not necessarily thriving

The term 'survivor' has heroic connotations: the person is still standing strong and resolute when the storm has passed. A survivor and a person demonstrating resilience are not necessarily undergoing the same process of recovery (from sexual abuse, for example). A survivor can be consumed with bitterness and blame while the resilient person is displaying personal growth and pursuing important goals (Walsh, 2006). As O'Connell Higgins (1994: 1) observes: 'Unlike the term *survivor*, *resilient* emphasizes that people do more than merely get through difficult emotional experiences, hanging on to inner equilibrium by a thread. Because *resilience* best captures the active *process* of self-righting and growth that characterizes some people so essentially' (original italics). The wonderfully expressive phrase 'self-righting' (Werner and Smith, 1982), much used by resilience writers, means to put your life back on track, including finding happiness again, after going through a period of upheaval or trauma. So a question I might want to ask a survivor is: Do you survive mostly happily or mostly miserably?

A former colleague of mine was going through some marital and professional difficulties and when asked how he was getting on he would reply, 'You know, hanging in there', followed by a grin and a merry quip such as: 'It could always be worse – my head could have fallen off!' However, in exploring the reality behind the reply, particularly after he had a couple of drinks in the pub, he would unleash a torrent of abuse at his wife and boss as the cause of all his problems. They had to change their ways before he could see any improvement in his current situation; he believed he was powerless to do anything about it himself. As time went on, he didn't need alcohol to reveal his true feelings, just anyone he could buttonhole. Not unexpectedly, he became professionally and socially isolated and eventually went off on sick leave. What distinguishes the resilient from the non-resilient is the struggle to find some way forward to a better future, whether this is through the support of others who are willing to help you and you are willing to receive it (but it would be unwise to accept help from those who remain embittered by their experiences), seeking professional help, digging deep inside yourself to uncover unexpected strengths, or a combination of all three. My colleague did not show any self-righting tendencies, only self-justifying, self-defeating beliefs and actions that kept him trapped within his unhappiness.

Struggling alone or seeking help?

In the previous paragraph, I mentioned whether you are willing to seek or receive help from others at a time of crisis in your life. If you pride yourself on your sturdy self-reliance, you might see help from others as a sign of weakness: 'People see me as a tower of strength. They come to me to help them sort out their problems. What will they think of me if I ask them for help?' (this person assumes that others see her in the same way she sees herself and therefore they would be shocked or derisive if she sought help from them). As Bonanno (2006: 33) points out: 'One of the misconceptions about resilience . . . is the idea that [it] is more or less found exclusively within the person.' In other words, self-righting is supposed to be achieved on your own. Nothing could be further from the truth (as I showed at the beginning of this chapter, one of the men who lost his job welcomed the support of family and friends while he looked for another one). Resilience is not developed in social isolation. If constructive support is being offered, take it. If you know that someone could provide valuable advice in your time of need, seek it. Such support and advice can reduce significantly the duration of your struggle to overcome your problems. Therefore, a balanced view of self-reliance includes both self- and social support.

Resilience and emotion

Resilience can be misconstrued as a form of stoicism, noble forbearance in the face of pain and suffering. To show emotion would be weakness of character and thereby impair or undermine your stoical stance. Resilience is actually about managing emotions, not suppressing them. To be fair to the ancient Stoic philosophers, their goal was not to live an emotionless life, but to learn how to experience fewer negative emotions (Irvine, 2009). If there appears to be no emotion in the face of adversity this may well signal incomplete processing of the experience and is likely to perpetuate poor, not resilient, responding to events. For example, Peter fell out with his adult son who threatened never to speak to him again. Peter's attitude to life's difficulties was always to 'roll with the punches'. 'If that's the way you want it son, then so be it. I'll always be here if you change your mind.' Friends were amazed at his calm demeanour in the face of his son's announcement; they assured him their own responses would be anything but calm.

However, two weeks later Peter flew into a rage in the high street when a man who looked very much like his son bumped into him. He later confessed that what his son had said to him 'hit me very hard indeed but I couldn't allow myself to feel it or others to see it until I bumped into that unfortunate man. I hope he'll forgive me wherever he is.' The only way that you can have an unemotional response to an event is if you truly don't care what has happened to you because the event has absolutely no significance for you. By definition, adversities are negative events which are likely to trigger negative emotions in you for the obvious reason that you didn't want these unpleasant events to occur in your life, so these emotions will need to be worked through in order to find adaptive responses to these events.

The popular image of bouncing back from adversity can give the impression of a joyous leap to safety from adversity's clutches. After all, 'bouncing back' does imply a quick and easy return from one's difficulties. For example, Janet, who liked to see herself as an upbeat person, came home to find that her flat had been burgled. Her flatmate, Sally, was very upset and kept crying. Janet was relieved that her valuables had not been stolen, nor had Sally's, so why can't she stop crying? Janet made herself a cup of coffee, surveyed the damage done to the flat and quietly complimented herself on feeling positive about what had happened: 'Just like me to look on the bright side.' A few nights later, Janet woke up in a panic thinking there was a burglar in the room. She took time off work, bewildered that she was acting in this 'shameful' way. Janet now felt on edge about experiencing another panic attack as well as the possibility of being burgled again. She was angry that her sense of privacy and security had been violated by the burglar and considered moving out. Sally had stopped crying and was coping better than her. Janet was eventually referred to a psychiatrist.

So resilience is not characterized by the absence of emotion or the presence of positive emotion. As the two above examples show, resilience involves experiencing negative emotions because bad things are happening to you. However, and this is a key point, since resilience depends on you being flexible when you respond to adverse events you are not stuck in your negative feelings. They do not paralyse you; they act as important sources of information that things are seriously awry in your life and need your attention (and it may take time for you to become attentive). For example, Simon was rejected by his girlfriend, felt gloomy, cried a lot, walked the streets at night trying to work out where the relationship had gone wrong, and listened interminably to the pop song 'She's Gone'. After a couple of weeks of feeling like this, he concluded that he had 'indulged myself enough' and a few weeks later was going out with a woman he had met at a dinner party.

As I shall discuss in Chapter 2, the way to moderate the intensity of your negative feelings is by modifying the thinking that drives these feelings. (A technical point about emotional change: it is hard to change negative feelings directly; it is usually done indirectly by changing your thoughts and behaviours; e.g. in depression, it is important to carry out daily behavioural activities which will help to lift your mood and provide you with a sense of accomplishment thereby changing your view that you're helpless.) In Simon's case, he stopped thinking that the end of the relationship was the end of his world; his world had indeed suffered a blow, but he got bored with feeling sorry for himself about it and wanted to 'get back in the game'. So negative emotions per se are not the problem: they only become problematic when they stop you from taking positive steps to change a situation (e.g. improving your performance at work) or adjusting constructively to it if it cannot be changed (e.g. you're sacked).

Resilience and behaviour

It's hard to know if you're thinking flexibly in the face of challenging circumstances unless there is behavioural evidence to support it; in other words, are you converting flexible attitudes into adaptable behaviour? For example, instead of always jumping to your own defence when you're criticized, you consider a range of options: asking for more information about your perceived deficiencies, walking away if appropriate, letting the criticism wash over you, practising relaxation skills when being criticized, asking for time to consider your reply, agreeing with those criticisms you consider to be true. However, nothing changes in practice as you continue to respond in exactly the same way. Your behavioural inflexibility probably means that you haven't really changed your thinking about the issue – 'How dare they criticize me! I'm not going to just stand there and take it.'

Behaviour can be divided into action tendencies (how you may or may not act in a situation) and completed or clear actions (what you actually did in a situation). This distinction is very important to make as resilience often involves you: (a) not doing what you want to do (e.g. watching the television) and (b) doing what you don't feel like doing (e.g. filling out forms). Developing resilience often means forgoing the pleasures of the moment in order to achieve longer term goals. For example, if you want to get fit but are not particularly enthusiastic about it, you might consider starting next week and then begin to reach for a book to read (action tendency) but change your mind – you go out for a run instead (clear action) as you remind yourself of what your longer term goal is.

Resilient response to adversity will often involve the experience of emotional pain and it can be very tempting to anaesthetize yourself to this pain with food, drink, drugs or other distractions. If you act on these action tendencies, you may well reduce or remove your pain in the moment but you will be storing up trouble for yourself in the longer term as you teach yourself that emotional pain is intolerable and therefore to be avoided whenever possible. Resilience is built through pain and struggle and the willingness, however reluctantly undertaken, to experience them. Non-resilient responding is the attempted avoidance of both. Without this reservoir of resilient attitudes and skills to draw from, future adversities will be much harder to deal with.

As resilience involves struggling to find a constructive way forward during tough times, you might believe that you have to win every struggle you are engaged in otherwise you're not demonstrating resilience and probably never will. This is more of the comic-book view of resilience. Like seeking to attain and maintain your ideal weight, being highly resilient is something to strive towards but is never perfectly executed at all times. It's highly unlikely you'll say one day, 'That's it. I've mastered resilience. Now, what's my next challenge?' Bearing this in mind, acting resiliently can be seen as a ratio between helpful and unhelpful behaviour in pursuit of your goals, for example, engaging in helpful behaviour 80 per cent of the time and engaging in unhelpful behaviour 20 per cent of the time. So resilience does involve acting non-resiliently at times, but it is important to ensure that your resilience balance sheet shows more assets (occurrences of helpful behaviour) than liabilities (occurrences of unhelpful behaviour).

For example, Diane described herself as 'very jealous, deeply distrustful of men'. Previous relationships had been destroyed through her incessant interrogation of her partners' behaviour for their presumed unfaithfulness (one had been). She described her current partner as 'wonderful' and wanted to learn to give him the benefit of the doubt that he was being faithful (unless there was good evidence to the contrary). Her struggle was to keep quiet instead of questioning her partner every time she had a suspicion, however slight, in order to develop a better relationship with him and channel her energies into more rewarding activities. In carrying out this plan, she was able to keep quiet 70 to 80 per cent of the time with a consequent improvement in the relationship and more of her time was now spent on studying for a college diploma: 'I feel more of a balanced person. I haven't felt like that in a long time. I'm hoping to get above 80 per cent.'

Distinguishing between what you can and cannot change

You cannot change how old you are but you can change which newspaper you read. That seems straightforward enough. If your partner leaves you and is definitely not coming back, you can decide to react differently to the situation by feeling sad about it rather than staying stuck and depressed. So your reaction is changeable, but your partner leaving you is unchangeable. Sadness allows you to process the loss of the relationship, thereby helping you to move on with your life. However, you might decide to try and change the unchangeable by attempting to get your partner back instead of moving on (e.g. sending emails to him, leaving messages on his voicemail, denying to yourself that it is over). Alternatively, you accept that the relationship is over but then believe that your depressed state is unchangeable and, instead of seeking professional help, try to manage it yourself through pills, alcohol and bed-hopping – activities which only intensify your low mood.

Now imagine that the relationship has broken down, but not irretrievably, and your partner will take you back under certain conditions. However, you cannot see that reconciliation is possible because of your depressed state. In order to see and act on this possibility, you first have to tackle your depression. In summary, what can and cannot be changed goes like this:

- If the situation (or aspects of it) can be changed, then take steps to do so.
- If the situation (or aspects of it) cannot be changed, then work on changing your emotional reaction.
- If the situation (or aspects of it) can be changed but your current level of emotional distress stops you from seeing this, then it is important to reduce your level of distress before you undertake any practical problem-solving steps.

Working out accurately which of these three positions reflects your present circumstances is not always easy to do. Therefore, seeking the views of respected others can help you clarify where you are in this process, as well as providing emotional support through these difficulties. Of course, there is another approach to problem solving which is to bury your head in the sand, thereby hoping the problem will go away or someone else will solve it for you. Even if you do adopt this strategy, you're still likely to feel the problem 'tapping on your shoulder' to remind you that it's still there. The longer problem solving is delayed, the more problems you're likely to face when you eventually pull your head out of the sand.

Resilience is ordinary, not extraordinary

This is good news. Grotberg (1999: 3) reassures us that 'resilience is not magic; it is not found only in certain people and it is not a gift from unknown sources. All humans have the capacity to become resilient'. However, if resilience is a universal capacity, not everyone will rush to learn how to develop it (see Chapter 3 for reasons why this reluctance might occur). There is no prescriptive way for people to be resilient. They can assemble their own resilience-building strategies depending on their personality styles, ages, individual strengths and cultural differences (Newman, 2003); in other words, customized resilience. For example, when I'm troubled I like to go for long walks to think things through and I usually return with my mood lifted and some problem-solving strategies emerging. My preference is to try and work things out on my own, but I will solicit others' opinions if I get stuck (relying only on my own ideas I would consider a non-resilient response to problem solving).

Turning adversity into advantage

This can read like a feel-good but empty slogan if you don't believe it, or an important truth if you do. Being able to find some positive meaning from your misfortune is a key factor in resilience. Timing is important in conveying this message: say it when someone is in the depths of despair and you will sound grossly insensitive; bring it up when she is making some headway in dealing with her difficulties and it will probably chime with her own awareness of herself as an evolving person, an unimagined potential emerging. As Joan said, 'When Geoffrey left me for that other woman I hated it, cried myself to sleep each night, drank too much, swore too much. How was I ever going to get over this? I've never been on my own. And yet six months later I don't mind living alone, it's not that bad. I didn't fall apart, or rather I did, but I didn't stay in pieces. I've sort of put myself back together again with the help of some dear friends. I'm certainly more independent and, amazingly, stronger than I ever thought I could be. If you had told me on the day Geoffrey left that I would get over this and emerge stronger from it, I would have sworn and then thrown something at you! I still wonder sometimes how on earth I got from there to here. I thought I could never be happy without him.' No life experience has to be wasted if you are open to learning from each one, but what is learnt usually emerges over the longer term, not immediately, as with Joan.

Drawing on a large body of research into how people cope with tragedy and trauma, Haidt (2006) suggests that people who have gone through dark times derive benefit from them in three principal ways. These benefits are collectively known as post-traumatic growth (Boniwell, 2006).

1 *Our self-image is changed.* Rising to meet the challenge of adversity can tap into unexpected abilities which change the way you see yourself – for example, from nervous insecurity to steady determination – which then, in turn, changes the way you view handling future difficulties: 'I'll be able to deal with them. I don't need to know exactly how I'll do it when the time comes; just the belief that I can do it is enough to make me feel confident.'

2 *The nature of our relationships is clarified and enriched.* We begin to see who are fair-weather friends and who are all-weather friends. This can be both a dispiriting and surprising experience: dispiriting because some presumed good friends are, strangely, no longer visiting or returning your phone calls, but surprising as friends you weren't particularly close to, or not too keen on in some cases, provide invaluable support during your term of trial. As well as sifting through friend-ships, enduring adversity helps to strengthen family bonds and draws you closer together: 'When my mum died in her early forties, I was devastated. My dad and me cried together, clung together to get through it. He told me things I'd never heard before about him and mum which made me laugh. I've never been so close to my dad.'

3 *Our priorities in life are altered.* It's as if your new perspective following the trauma has cut a swathe through your life removing anything that is seen as unimportant; your brush with death has made you acutely aware that time is precious and you do not want to waste this irreplaceable resource: 'Before the car accident I took my family for granted. I kept on saying I would spend more time with them instead of working so hard, but I never got round to it. They were always there when I got home, so what's the fuss? Work was the battle-ground to prove myself. Since the accident, I've got round to it and apologized for my distance as a father and husband. Family life has never been better and rising through the ranks at work just doesn't have the same appeal now. I feel sorry for those who see succeeding at work as a life-or-death struggle, but it took the accident to open up my eyes to what I was missing in my life.'

Looking beyond adversity

So far in this chapter, I have been talking about resilience in the context of adversity, but the discussion of resilience has been expanded by some writers and researchers 'to become a primary focus of each person's life, whether or not that person has experienced great adversity. All of us encounter some degree of stress and challenge in everyday life. No one can predict which of us will at some point face unimagined adversity' (Brooks and Goldstein, 2003: 3). The Hardiness Institute in California, a consulting and training organization, was founded to 'teach people attitudes and skills that make them resilient under stress' (Maddi and Khoshaba, 2005: 5). I run resilience training programmes for mental health professionals, coaches and businesspeople. Resilience skills are taught in some schools – adding a fourth R to the traditional three Rs (Papházy, 2003).

Reivich and Shatté (2003) suggest that resilience is not just about struggling with setbacks (reactive) but also focuses on reaching out to others to improve our relationships, finding new friends and sexual partners, taking risks like becoming self-employed and enjoying life to the full (proactive). Reaching out is itself a risk – you might be rejected or experience failure. However, if you can learn to separate specific life failures from self-condemnation about these failures ('My business failed, but I'm not a failure as person') and not follow other rejection – your new partner drops you after a week – with self-rejection ('My worth as a person stays constant whatever happens to me, so the presence or absence of a relationship in my life does affect my level of enjoyment, but not my worth'), then reaching out is likely to be anticipated eagerly rather than undertaken reluctantly. It is this expanded discussion of resilience that is the focus of this book.

Defining resilience

Given the detailed discussion of resilience that I've presented, it would not do justice to the subject to sum it up succinctly but inaccurately along the usual 'bouncing back' lines. Therefore I have developed with my colleague, Professor Windy Dryden of London University, a lengthy definition of resilience (see Box 1.1) which takes into account some of the points discussed in this chapter as well as distilling our collective experience as CBT

What is resilience? Neenan and Dryden's view

Resilience comprises a set of flexible cognitive, behavioural and emotional responses to acute or chronic adversities which can be unusual or commonplace. These responses can be learned and are within the grasp of everyone; resilience is not a rare quality given to a chosen few. While many factors affect the development of resilience, the most important one is the attitude you adopt to deal with adversity. Therefore, attitude (meaning) is the heart of resilience.

Resilience, as commonly understood, refers to 'bouncing back' from adversity. A more detailed and realistic understanding of resilience involves you frequently experiencing pain and struggle while coming back rather than bouncing back from misfortune. This experience of pain and struggle does not stop you from working to change those adversities that can be changed or adjusting constructively to those adversities that cannot be changed. Nor does the experience of pain and struggle stop you from moving towards your goals, however slowly or falteringly, or pursuing what is important to you. This forward movement is a defining feature of resilience. As such, being resilient does not restore the status quo in your life prior to the adversity – springing back to the way it was – but, rather, what you have learned from tackling the adversity changes you for the better and helps you to become more keenly aware of what is important in your life and, as we said, encourages you to pursue it.

While resilience is the response of you as an individual, its development can be facilitated or impaired by the context in which you live such as, respectively, having supportive friends or experiencing violence from your partner. Thus, resilience is best understood by taking in the wider context of your life rather than focusing on purely internal factors like optimism or self-discipline. Finally, the focus of resilience has been widened to include teaching people attitudes and skills to help them deal better with the challenges of daily living, but what's been learnt also acts as preparation for the inevitable adversities that lie ahead.

therapists. A couple of points about the definition need clarifying. In the first paragraph, 'acute or chronic adversities' refers, respectively, to those events that are short-lived (e.g. stuck overnight in winter in a traffic jam on the M25) and those of long duration (e.g. coping with Alzheimer's disease). 'Unusual or commonplace adversities' are, respectively, those that are dramatic and often capture world attention such as terrorist bombings or earthquakes, and the everyday events that most of us experience such as job loss, relationship break-up and interpersonal conflict. Finally, 'attitude' is pinpointed as the heart of resilience which is the subject of the next chapter.

Chapter 2

Attitude
The heart of resilience

Introduction

'Attitude is very consequential stuff. It determines everything one does, from falling in love to voting for one candidate rather than another,' says the philosopher Anthony Grayling (2005: 23). What is an attitude? Attitudes are relatively enduring evaluations (positive or negative) you make of an object, person, group, issue or concept (e.g. 'I hate political correctness!'; 'I like people who are optimistic'; 'We should all be concerned about global warming'). Attitudes have three components:

- *thoughts* – what you think about the person (in this case): 'I can't trust him'
- *emotions* – how you feel about the person: 'I get angry about his shifty behaviour'
- *behaviour* – how you act towards the person: 'I always keep him at arm's length'.

When I talk about attitudes the emphasis will be on thinking as this powerfully influences how we feel and behave (throughout the book I will be using the terms attitudes and beliefs interchangeably). Though thoughts, feelings and behaviours do influence each other in an interdependent relationship (e.g. if I wake up depressed and stay in bed most of the day this is likely to strengthen my view that 'I can't do anything to change how I feel'), thinking is the 'senior partner' in this interdependent relationship. What we think (i.e. the content of our thinking) and how we think (i.e. how we process information to arrive at our conclusions) are the particular concerns of cognitive behavioural therapists.

Resilient attitudes are flexible in nature in order to adapt to new circumstances: accepting (but not passively) that an adversity has occurred, distinguishing between what is and what isn't within your control to change, and trying out different problem-solving solutions. Do remember that flexible attitudes are not endlessly flexible: you will eventually bump up against their limits, but before you do so you're likely to have experienced considerable room for manoeuvre in your decision making. For example, if I lose a valued friendship I'm not going to feel happy about it (even if I wanted to). I will feel sad about this loss but also realize that new and meaningful friendships can be found. I will avoid descending into depression because I will not view my life as empty and bleak without his friendship. Rigid attitudes by definition are not adaptable and, therefore, your struggle to overcome adversity is likely to be longer and harder until such time as you allow other problem-solving perspectives into your thinking. Attitude change may come from the attempts of others to change your mind or you can initiate the process yourself or it might be a combination of both processes (as the philosopher Roger Scruton remarked, the best evidence you have a mind is when you change it).

Writing about resilience doesn't stop me from acting in self-defeating ways. For example, I had a lumbar disc prolapse in 1997. I was in great pain and my mobility was considerably restricted. I spent most of my time resting in my flat. I was unable to go out and buy food (I lived alone) and I consumed mostly soup and bread. My brother and his wife lived close by and kept insisting I should stay with them until I was on my feet again. I declined their offer, equally insisting that I was coping well enough on my own, but I wasn't. I had accepted my back condition, followed doctor's orders to rest and take tablets to control the pain and muscle spasms but, stupidly and rigidly, I clung to the idea that I would be a burden if I stayed with them (I knew this was untrue) and, even worse, that suffering in solitude was somehow good for my character – tested and not found wanting – and to accept my brother's invitation was a sign of weakness and surrender. His daily phone calls urging me to change my mind prompted a vigorous self-debate with my 'suffering in solitude' arguments. After several days, reason prevailed over rigidity and I moved in with him. The benefits of doing so were soon apparent.

From the CBT perspective of developing resilience, how you think about the unpleasant events that happen to you largely determines how you feel about and behave towards these events. As Reivich and Shatté (2003: 11) state:

> Our research has demonstrated that the number-one road-block to resilience is not genetics, not childhood experiences, not a lack of opportunity or wealth. The principal obstacle to tapping into our inner strength lies with our cognitive [thinking] style – ways of looking at the world and interpreting events that every one of us develops from childhood.

Modern research confirms an ancient truth as stated by the Stoic philosopher and patron saint of the resilient, Epictetus (c. AD 55–135): 'Men are disturbed not by the things which happen, but by the opinions about the things' (trans., Long, 2004: 3). In other words, events don't disturb us: we disturb ourselves only by the views we hold about these events. Epictetus's viewpoint can seem extreme to modern ears (and some ancient ears too) and doesn't ring completely true. For example, if you're suddenly hit in the face by someone wielding a baseball bat, this is likely to shatter any inner peace you might be experiencing, irrespective of your view about being hit in the face (you probably won't have time to formulate a view, so quick and sudden is the attack). Your view-point will come into focus in the aftermath of the attack: from how you cope with this brutal disruption to your life and the physical pain to facing your attacker in court (if he is caught and prose-cuted). This is the more realistic challenge of Epictetus's insight. I think there is much to be gained from reading the Stoic philos-ophers: 'The Stoic philosophy of life may be old, but it merits the attention of any modern individual who wishes to have a life that is both meaningful and fulfilling – who wishes, that is, to have a good life' (Irvine, 2009: 4). The human condition is little changed in 2000 years and the advice the Stoics offered then is still relevant today.

Gaining an ABC education

Where you're looking is usually where your attention is. Your attention is usually on what's going on in the external world rather than focused on what's going on in your internal world, and you're probably not considering how these two worlds might be connected when you feel upset. My clients frequently point to events or other people as the cause of their problems without reflecting on how their own beliefs and attitudes might also be implicated in contributing to these problems. In CBT parlance, this is known as A→C thinking and here is an example of it:

> **A = activating event or adversity**: becoming tongue-tied and blushing while giving a presentation to a group of colleagues, some of whom then laugh at you.

$$\downarrow$$

> **C = consequences**: emotional – anger (held in), embarrassment, anxiety; behavioural – try to calm yourself down, lean on the table for support and smile weakly at the audience (hoping to convey that you are enjoying the laughter as well).

You might say, 'Who wouldn't be upset if they were laughed at?' Your viewpoint allows for no individual variation to the same event: the laughter itself 'makes' you upset; even if you didn't want to feel upset, the laughter wouldn't 'allow' you to have any other reaction. The problem with A→C thinking is that it assumes we are passive recipients of whatever happens to us in life instead of being active meaning-makers, trying to make sense of what is happening to us by assigning meaning (good, bad or indifferent) to events. Persisting with A→C thinking is likely to keep you in a state of helplessness as you believe you can only feel and act differently once events at A change in your favour (e.g. you feel relieved when your boss says you don't have to do any more presentations).

Another argument advanced to support A→C thinking (and the flip side of the one above) is that when good things happen to you then you will feel good. That seems logical, you might say. The reason you would feel good about good events is because you appraise these events in a positive way. Just imagine someone you really fancy says 'yes' when you ask him for a date, 'I'm over the moon. He's fantastic, and he's going out with me!' However, you quickly learn he has some very unsavoury personal habits and your enthusiasm for him rapidly wanes, 'He's not so fantastic after all.' Your feelings about him change because your opinion of him has changed based on the new information you've acquired. You can't make yourself still feel highly positive about him (or you're going to have a tough time trying) when your viewpoint has changed so dramatically. What's missing from A→C thinking is the crucial importance of the B, your evaluation of events at A. CBT uses a simple model, ABC, to demonstrate how your thinking powerfully influences how you feel and behave when faced with adverse events. To return to the above example:

A = activating event or adversity: becoming tongue-tied and blushing while giving a presentation to a group of colleagues, some of whom then laugh at you.
B = beliefs and attitudes you hold about what happened at A: 'How dare they laugh at me! I look like an incompetent fool. My credibility has been destroyed along with any respect they had for me.'
C = consequences: emotional – anger (held in), embarrassment, anxiety; behavioural – try to calm yourself down, lean on the table for support and smile weakly at the audience (hoping to convey that you are enjoying the laughter as well).

Now we have a much better understanding of why you would be so upset at C once we know what you were thinking at B. If we return to the same situation in the ABC model, different consequences at C can be achieved by changing your viewpoint at B about A:

A = activating event or adversity: becoming tongue-tied and blushing while giving a presentation to a group of colleagues, some of whom then laugh at you.
B = beliefs and attitudes you hold about what happened at A: 'I don't like becoming tongue-tied but I'm determined to keep going when they've stopped laughing. Let them have their fun if they wish. I want to improve my presentational skills including staying calm under pressure. Their laughter is giving me the chance to practise these skills.'
C = consequences: emotional – annoyance mixed with satisfaction; behavioural – stand quietly until the laughter has died down.

Within the context of the ABC model, it is of fundamental importance to develop B→C thinking (i.e. that your view of events, not the events themselves, largely determines your emotional and behavioural reactions) if you want to develop greater resilience. B→C thinking encourages you to take responsibility for how you respond to events, thereby becoming the author of your life experiences ('She left me but my life is still interesting to me, with or without her'). A→C thinking will keep you trapped in non-resilient responding to events as you believe your life experiences are being written for you by forces outside of your control ('She made my life nothing when she left me'). It is also important when using the ABC model not to dwell on how you feel at C or engage in long explanations of what happened at A; get to the B promptly (if possible) as this is the most important element of the model to understand and start working on.

For example, Brian felt intimidated when talking to his boss as she was well educated, articulate, conveyed her opinions forcefully and seemed supremely self-confident. He was clearly engaging in A→C thinking when he said, 'She makes me feel intimidated.' If I hadn't interrupted him, he would have continued with his lengthy psychological profile of her to explain the cause of his problems. I asked him something very different. 'How do you intimidate *yourself* in her presence?' (attempting to elicit his B→C thinking). He was somewhat mystified by this question and said he didn't intimidate himself, she did. I asked him how he viewed his own educational achievements. 'A few O levels, not too bright I suppose.' Then I asked him about his own level of articulacy ('Too many ers and ums, sound unconfident'), conveying his opinions ('Cautiously, probably ready to change them if someone objects strongly to them'), and to estimate his own level of self-confidence ('Not very high'). By looking at how he saw himself, he realized he brought this sense of mental defeat to every encounter with her. So if he wanted to feel more confident, less intimidated, in her presence he would need to change the way he viewed himself. So a good rule of thumb in developing resilience is this: manage yourself first in order to have a more constructive response to events whether or not this leads to others altering their behaviour as a result of your changes.

In Brian's case, he discovered that he was always 'falling short' in his estimation of himself: 'I should be better educated, more articulate and confident. I should be able stick to my opinions if I believe in them. I should be able to stand up for myself more.' This 'falling short' focus (from the ideal 'should' to the reality of his actual performance) just perpetuated his belief in his own inferiority. By changing the focus to establish a baseline of workplace competences (i.e. behaviours he carried out competently), Brian was able to see that improvement was possible ('moving up' instead of 'falling short') through belief change based on self-acceptance (e.g. 'I'm equal to others in terms of human worth, but not in terms of skills') and skills practice (e.g. in assertiveness). Though he was never completely at ease with his boss during their meetings, he liked to see them as a laboratory where he could try out his new ways of thinking and acting. Just imagine the longer term consequences for Brian if he continued to believe that he couldn't change unless his boss did first (he said she stayed the same).

Encouraging new thinking

All this talk about changing perspectives, attitudes or viewpoints can give the impression that it's easy to do, like going into a supermarket, finding the 'attitudes shelf' and picking one ('I will be confident at all times') to become your new instant outlook. Needless to say, it takes work and effort to adopt a new attitude. There are a number of steps to follow in this adoption process.

Step 1: Where are you stuck in your thinking about your difficulties?

Think of a situation you're struggling with. What beliefs do you hold that might be making the struggle harder to deal with? For example, Janice had her own successful business but was reluctant to delegate important work to her staff just in case they did a poor job and then she would have to take it back and do it herself, so why give it to them in the first place? Additionally, she closely monitored their routine work to spot and correct the mistakes they were making which could harm her business. Her 'stuck' belief was: 'I must be certain they can do what is expected of them without my business suffering if they get things wrong' ('musts' can be seen as tyrannical, suppressing other viewpoints). Janice often experienced physical and emotional exhaustion, including sleepless nights, in her efforts to keep the business running smoothly.

Step 2: What belief would you like to hold?

It is very important to consider how you would like to respond to the situation in order to contrast it with your current response. You're unlikely to give up your old ideas unless you have new ones to replace them. You can run through in your imagination how you would like to think, feel and behave in that situation. Make your new responses as vivid as possible. Janice's alternative belief was: 'I want to coach my staff to develop their potential by giving them more responsibility and ease the burdens on myself as well as learning to tolerate the uncertainty of not knowing immediately what effect this new management style will have on my business.' She was apprehensive about 'stepping back' but could see the benefits of doing so, such as 'spending more time on thinking strategically where I would like the business to be in the next few years as well as getting back to a peaceful sleep routine'.

Step 3: Examining old and new beliefs

New beliefs create new possibilities for your life, but the old beliefs still remain strong and ready to intrude into your life and block your progress. They don't wither away overnight and are not forced out of your mind for good by the mere presence of the new beliefs. To begin both to weaken your conviction in the old beliefs and strengthen your conviction in the new ones, both beliefs can be examined along the following lines.

Is your belief rigid or flexible?

Rigid beliefs keep you committed to a fixed viewpoint even if the results you are getting are self-defeating. You're a prisoner of your beliefs (McKay and Fanning, 1991). In contrast, flexible beliefs allow you to adapt to changing circumstances by experimenting with new ways of doing things – a personal growth mindset (Dweck, 2006). Janice could see that her old belief was rigid and the new one was flexible. However, she was curious to know why she thought in this rigid way. While some discussion can be helpful (e.g. 'We are all prone to think rigidly, particularly when we are under pressure or emotionally upset'), it is important not to dwell on this issue as the focus is on *how* to tackle rigid thinking, not trying to discover *why* it exists in the first place (it just does in all of us).

Is your belief realistic or unrealistic?

Does your subjective view of the situation correspond with the facts of the situation? For example, you have missed your train (fact) but insist that you should have caught it; you were stuck in a traffic jam on the way to the station (fact) but insist that the traffic jam shouldn't have been there; and you overslept (fact) but insist that you should have woken up at the usual time. There is a wide gap between the facts and your view of them that is likely to make your emotional and behavioural reaction more intense and longer lasting (e.g. you're angry and agitated for most of the morning after missing the train).

Janice's rigid belief – 'I must be certain they can do what is expected of them without my business suffering if they get things wrong' – wasn't realistic because she couldn't be certain of the outcome until after her staff had completed the delegated tasks and she had spent a period of time watching for any adverse effects on her business if she failed to spot and correct any mistakes they had made. These things she couldn't know in advance. Her flexible belief based on coaching her staff to improve their performance was realistic. She said it was likely that they could execute the delegated tasks successfully and unlikely that her business would suffer grievously if they made mistakes. Also, she would be able to tolerate the uncertainty attached to introducing a new management approach. It was also likely, she said, that moving from an overly controlling managerial style to a coaching one would produce the personal benefits she hoped for.

Is your belief helpful or unhelpful?

This looks at the practical consequences of holding on to your belief. Are you getting more advantages or disadvantages from maintaining the belief? If the belief is giving you poor results, why would you want to hang on to it? To this question Janice replied, 'I suppose I worry that if I step back and give them more responsibility and don't interfere so much, something might go horribly wrong.' So there was an advantage in keeping the old belief. On the other hand, the disadvantages of keeping it were many and we filled a whiteboard in my office with them, such as feeling intense pressure all day long and being unable to switch off when she got home. The advantages of coaching her staff to improve their performance included being able to focus on important strategic issues for the business and reducing her hours at the office. The one possible disadvantage was that she would now have to put her new belief into practice and wait apprehensively to see what happened.

Would you teach your belief to others?

If you think your belief is reasonable – it makes good sense to you – would you teach it to others like your children, partner, friends or colleagues? For example, if you believe that making mistakes means you're a failure as a person, would you teach this to your children? If no, what would you teach them instead and what prevents you from teaching this to yourself as well? If yes, what might be the consequences for them of adopting your belief? What would it be like to live in a world where everyone had your belief? I asked Janice to imagine running a workshop for businesspeople on 'Coaching to improve performance'. Would she teach the audience that they must be *absolutely* certain their staff can do what's expected of them before they delegate important tasks and thereby increase their own burdens in the meantime while waiting for this certainty to arrive? She replied that holding this belief would cause great inefficiency in the workplace and therefore she wouldn't teach it. She said that using coaching, giving people the opportunity to show you what they are capable of, including correcting and learning from their own mistakes, is the way to develop both her staff and business.

From insight to action

Gaining insight into the crucial role your beliefs and attitudes play in powerfully influencing your feelings and behaviours is not enough to bring about change or, more precisely, deep and lasting change. Think of the time you may have said of an unproductive behaviour, 'So that's why I do that. How very interesting. That's going to help me a lot.' But several days later this insight is not so 'interesting' and your enthusiasm for change rapidly wanes as you contemplate unenthusiastically the effort required to change this behaviour. The working through part of the change process requires that your new knowledge now needs to be put into action, preferably on a daily basis, in order to strengthen your conviction in it. Acting to support your new beliefs and acting against the old ones can feel strange, like deciding from today that you're always going to put your right leg into your trousers first when, for as long as you can remember, the left leg went in first. This 'feeling strange' phase is to be expected and will eventually pass if you persevere with your change efforts (old habits may now seem unfamiliar). So remember: 'If it ain't strange, it ain't change!' (Neenan and Dryden, 2002a).

Janice began to delegate some important tasks to her staff (remembering that she kept overall control of these tasks) and interfered much less in monitoring their routine work. She did experience a 'push–pull' tension from time to time: pushing herself to micromanage the delegated tasks when she was feeling anxious that not being 'personally on top of things at all times' would mean business failure, but then forcefully reminding herself of her new coaching outlook and pulling herself back to get on with her own work. As I discussed in Chapter 1 under the heading 'Resilience and behaviour' (pp. 11–12), it is important that the ratio between resilient and non-resilient behaviour is heavily weighted towards the former behaviour so that your resilience balance sheet shows more assets than liabilities. In Janice's case, the ratio was 75 per cent to 25 per cent in favour of her new belief. Staff morale and performance improved once they felt they could be trusted to do a competent job, and Janice spent most of her time on the key managerial functions of running a business. Her staff inevitably made mistakes but her business did not suffer in any appreciable way.

Maintaining change

Once the change you desire has been achieved, the next stage is to maintain it. Imagine exercising hard to develop a washboard stomach, then stopping the exercise because you believe your stomach muscles will now remain firm without any further assistance from you. So in order to guard against your changes decaying through your neglect of maintaining them and, consequently, your old self-defeating beliefs and behaviours regaining their dominance in your life, you need to develop a maintenance message. It can be something simple to encapsulate your new outlook such as in Janice's case: 'Coaching my staff, not controlling them'. Every day at work she would take a few minutes to review whether she was adhering to her new outlook, what changes might be needed in her relationships with her staff, and gaining regular feedback from them on this new way of working.

'I'm more in tune with my feelings than my thoughts'

Earlier in this chapter I asked you to pinpoint where you're stuck in your thinking, as this provides an entry point into understanding how well or badly you are struggling with your current difficulties. Some of you might say: 'I know how I feel, but I'm not sure what I think.' Understanding how you feel can reveal what you're thinking – your feelings are driven by your beliefs. Emotions contain themes that point to possible beliefs you might hold (see Table 2.1).

When you are upset, try to work out which emotion you might be feeling and listen for the beliefs that are 'speaking to you'. The themes in Table 2.1 can orient you to what these emotions and accompanying beliefs might be. It is through belief change that emotional change is largely achieved. It is important not to confuse thoughts with feelings, that is, using the word 'feel' does not turn the statement into a genuine emotion (e.g. 'I feel everyone is against me'; 'I feel I'll never overcome this problem'; 'I feel I don't get enough help from my colleagues'; 'I feel let down by my partner because she didn't take my side when I was arguing with the next-door neighbour'). These are all examples of thoughts, not feelings. You might believe you have dozens of 'feelings' if you insert the word 'feel' into every sentence. Therefore, when you say you're not sure what your thoughts are, they're usually there but masquerading

Table 2.1 Emotions, themes and possible beliefs

Emotion	Theme	Possible belief
Anxiety	Threat or danger.	'I can't cope on my own if he leaves me.'
Depression	Significant loss, failure.	'I'm worthless without a job.'
Guilt	Moral lapse, hurting others.	'I'm a bad father for shouting at my children.'
Anger	Personal rules violated, frustration.	'You shouldn't interrupt me when I'm speaking!'
Shame	Perceived weakness or defect revealed to others.	'I'm a pathetic wimp for crying in front of my colleagues.'
Hurt	Let down or treated badly (and you don't deserve to be treated in this way).	'You didn't stand by me when I really needed you. I've always stood by you.'
Envy	Covet good fortune of others.	'I wanted that promotion. I hope he chokes on his success.'
Jealousy	Threat to present relationship posed by another person.	'He's so good looking. I bet he could seduce my girlfriend if he wanted to and she would want him to.'

as feelings. The four examples of 'feelings' already mentioned should all read, 'I believe'. If you look at Table 2.1, the statement 'I believe I've been let down by my partner because she didn't take my side when I was arguing with the next-door neighbour' is likely to indicate you are feeling hurt and/or angry (hurt often lies behind anger). If you continue to see thoughts as feelings 'you obscure the real feelings that are related to those thoughts' (Gilson and Freeman, 1999: 46).

Let's go a step further. You can pinpoint how you behave, not how you think or feel. Each of the emotions in Table 2.1 is connected to a behaviour.

Emotion	Behaviour
Anxiety	Trying to avoid a threat or danger
Depression	Withdrawing from pleasurable activities
Guilt	Begging for forgiveness
Anger	Verbal and/or physical aggression
Shame	Hiding, withdrawing, not meeting the gaze of others
Hurt	Withdrawing (sulking)
Envy	Trying to undermine others' good fortune
Jealousy	Monitoring and questioning your partner's behaviour

Let's see how beliefs, emotions and behaviour are closely linked. For example, if you are procrastinating (behaviour) over asking someone out, what are you avoiding? You're likely to feel anxious (emotion) if you ask him out because he might say 'no'. What would be the meaning you attach to the word 'no'? 'I'm unattractive and no one wants me' (belief). This belief, like any belief that is troubling you, can be examined by using the four ways listed earlier in this chapter: is your belief rigid or flexible, realistic or unrealistic, helpful or unhelpful, and would you teach it to others? So, returning to your procrastination, this behaviour protects you, in your mind, from feared rejection and subsequent self-denigration. What this behaviour does not do is help you to develop a resilient response to this specific situation as well as, if you continue with your general avoidant behaviour, whatever comes your way in life. That you can learn to deal with anything in life was the profound and inspiring message of the late Viktor Frankl.

Hope amid despair

The Austrian psychiatrist and psychotherapist Viktor Frankl (1905–1997) survived the horrors of four concentration camps including Auschwitz and famously wrote that 'everything can be taken from a man but one thing: the last of the human freedoms – to choose one's attitude in any given set of circumstances, to choose one's own way' (1985: 86). This viewpoint can be traced back to Epictetus and other Stoic philosophers. Choosing one's attitude is your responsibility and this task cannot be given to someone else to do for you. Frankl saw that those who gave meaning to their lives, even in the most wretched of circumstances, were the most likely to survive; those prisoners who lost faith in the future were doomed, he observed. The worst of circumstances could bring out the best in human nature such as some prisoners giving away their last piece of bread to help others. He also saw behaviour of the most depraved kind. Witnessing the best and worst in human behaviour, he realized that both these potential behaviours reside in all of us and which one is acted upon depends on the decisions we make, not the circumstances we find ourselves in (decisions, not conditions, as Frankl pithily remarked). Frankl's book, *Man's Search for Meaning* from which the above quote comes, has never been out of print since it was first published in 1946. It is considered to be one of the most influential books of the twentieth century (Redsand, 2006).

As a result of Frankl's experiences in the camps he developed a psychotherapy called logotherapy which helps people to find meaning in their lives when they might otherwise give up: 'Meaning is the primary motivational force in man' (Frankl, 1985: 121). Frankl emphasized that it is not important to search for the meaning of life in general 'but rather the specific meaning of a person's life at any given moment' (1985: 131). Meaning can be found in life 'even up to the last moment, the last breath' (Frankl, 1997: 64). To really think about what it means to choose your attitude in any given situation, Pattakos (2008) suggests that you pick a situation which you are having a hard time with and write down ten *positive* things about it without imposing any constraints on your imagination (when he was first introduced to this exercise, he had to find ten positive things about dying today). This exercise, though usually difficult to do, confronts you with the possibility of finding new perspectives as you learn to engage in 'the last of the human freedoms'.

One of my clients, Lucy, dreaded living alone – 'It didn't work when I tried it before' – but knew that her current turbulent relationship was coming to an end. She considered the possibility of trying it again. When I explained the rationale for the ten positive things exercise, she replied, 'You mean ten lousy things!' When she tried in the session to think of even one positive thing, her mind went blank. 'This is bloody hard to do.' It was important that I did not supply a list of ten things I considered would benefit her as this would rob the exercise of its potency: the meaning of living alone had to come from her, not me. She said she would try and come up with some ideas before the next session. At the next session, she read out her ten positive things:

1 Get pissed without my boyfriend complaining.
2 Walk around the house naked without snide comments being made about my body.
3 Try to be more independent.
4 Take stock of my life.
5 Have the bed all to myself.
6 Try and get on with myself a bit better.
7 Have my girlfriends round for a good laugh without my boyfriend giving me threatening looks.
8 Stay in the bath for as long as I want.
9 Get myself a dog. I always wanted a dog.
10 Play my music whenever I want to.

While hardly over the moon about the prospect of living alone, the possibilities she had dragged out of herself encouraged her to be a little more optimistic that it could work this time. At the follow-up appointments, agreed at the end of therapy, she said living alone 'wasn't too bad after all and I'm getting stronger within myself' and she wasn't in any rush to find a new partner. Whether living alone or facing a terminal illness, positive meaning can be extracted from these experiences if you're prepared to search for it.

The will behind the power

I mentioned earlier in the chapter the importance of Epictetus's dictum – 'People are not disturbed by events but by their views of these events' – as the foundation of a resilient outlook. A passionate devotee of Epictetus's doctrines was James Stockdale (1923–

2005), a navy pilot shot down over North Vietnam in 1965. As he was parachuting to earth and contemplating the prospect of long imprisonment, he whispered to himself, 'I'm leaving the world of technology and entering the world of Epictetus' (Stockdale, 1993: 7). Stockdale endured seven and a half years of imprisonment as a prisoner of war, including torture and long periods of solitary confinement. He went into captivity with a broken leg and even though it was crudely operated on he was in pain for several years. Stockdale frequently consoled himself with Epictetus's dictum (he had memorized many of them): 'Lameness is an impediment to the leg, but not to the will [Epictetus was lame]. And add this reflection on the occasion of everything that happens; for you will find it an impediment to something else, but not to yourself' (trans., Long, 2004: 4).

Stockdale attributed to Epictetus's teachings his ability to endure captivity and return home physically debilitated but psychologically intact (Stockdale, 1993). Sherman (2005: 6) called his Epictetan experiment 'empowerment in enslavement'. He was much in demand as a speaker; his central theme was how to prevail with dignity when facing adversity, whether in war or peace.

Light in her darkness

Helen Keller (1880–1968) lost her sight and hearing when she was 19 months old. She was taught to speak, read and write by a teacher, Annie Sullivan. Helen grew up to become an author, lecturer and advocate for people with disabilities. She also supported other progressive causes such as women's suffrage, workers' rights, birth control and racial desegregation. Her stance on these issues made enemies – not everyone saw her as a saint. She believed that though she couldn't see or hear the world, this shouldn't prevent her from commenting upon what was going on within it (Herrmann, 1999). She was seen by many people around the world as an inspiring role model in overcoming such seemingly insurmountable disabilities. Though the temptation to succumb to a life of pessimism was great, she resisted it (she said that no pessimist ever opened a new doorway for the human spirit):

> Sometimes, it is true, a sense of isolation enfolds me like a cold mist as I sit alone and wait at life's shut gate. Beyond there is light, and music, and sweet companionship; but I may not

enter. Fate, silent, pitiless, bars the way . . . but my tongue will not utter the bitter, futile words that rise to my lips, and they fall back into my heart like unshed tears. Silence sits immense upon my soul. Then comes hope with a smile and whispers, 'There is joy in self-forgetfulness.' So I try to make the light in others' eyes my sun, the music in others' ears my symphony, the smile on others' lips my happiness.

(Keller, 1903/2007: 64–65)

These three extraordinary individuals – Viktor Frankl, James Stockdale and Helen Keller – have much to teach us that can be applied to our own lives: principally, that we have the ability to develop an inner freedom from despair and thereby face whatever confronts us in life with courage, determination and dignity. Having written these words, I am reminded of what I said in Chapter 1 that resilience is not the special gift of an extraordinary few but, rather, a capacity open to all of us to develop.

Finding meaning in the moment

In 2007 I had arranged to run a two-day CBT course in Kent. One of my back teeth had been troubling me for a few days prior to the course (unbeknown to me it had split and an abscess had formed). When I got to the hotel late on Sunday night I had severe toothache. I knew I wasn't going to cancel the course and return home (there was no one else to run it for me). I wanted to honour my commitments as well as find some way of tolerating the pain. The earliest I could get to my dentist would be on Wednesday. I thought of Frankl's point about choosing your attitude in any given set of circumstances. What was my attitude going to be? I picked Epictetus's dictum so beloved by James Stockdale: 'Lameness is an impediment to the leg but not to the will.' Mine became: 'Toothache is an impediment to my peace of mind but not to me running the course.' I had little sleep, didn't eat much, and experienced sharp stabs of pain every time my teeth touched. I did notice that the pain was less intense when teaching the course – distraction I presume – but most intense late at night in the hotel when distractions were few apart from going out for yet another walk. Driving home on Tuesday evening I felt a quiet satisfaction that I had prevailed over the pain; becoming reluctantly used to it but also knowing what increased or decreased its intensity. I had one more night to go. I was extremely happy the next day when the dentist yanked out the tooth and my pain rapidly disappeared.

The heart examined

If you accept the premise that your attitudes shape your responses to events, then identifying what they are can reveal whether you're acting resiliently or self-defeatingly in the face of adversity. The cognitive behavioural therapy model ABC provides you with a structured way of finding out what your attitudes are. You don't have to stay with your current viewpoint, no matter how long you've subscribed to it. Other more potentially helpful perspectives can be explored if you're prepared to expend the time and effort in seeking them out. Unfortunately, some individuals find it very difficult to shift their viewpoint or even to want to. Some of these resilience-blocking beliefs are discussed in the next chapter.

Chapter 3

Attitudes that undermine resilience building

Introduction

Resilience is one of the subjects studied by positive psychologists. Positive psychology was launched in the late 1990s and focuses on identifying and building on your strengths and virtues (what's right with you) rather than looking at your deficits and weaknesses (what's wrong with you) which has been the remit of traditional psychology:

> People want more than just to correct their weaknesses. They want lives imbued with meaning, and not just to fidget until they die. Lying awake at night, you probably ponder, as I do, how to go from plus two to plus seven in your life, not just how to go from minus five to minus three and feel a little less miserable day by day.
>
> (Seligman, 2003: xi)

It seems that both forms of psychology are required for personal growth: traditional psychology to get you from minus five or three to nought (e.g. overcoming social shyness and a tendency towards reclusiveness) and then positive psychology to get you from nought to plus five or seven (e.g. building social networks, feeling self-confident and leading a more enjoyable life). Some psychologists suggest it's 'simply psychology', not traditional or positive, if it 'spans the whole of the human condition, from disorder and distress to well-being and fulfilment' (Linley et al., 2006: 6).

Being resilient is definitely a strength, but in order to help you develop it we first need to know what blocks its development and what can be done to remove these blocks. What follows are some attitudes that keep people trapped in non-resilient ways of responding to life's ups and downs (these attitudes are not the only or key ones that interfere with resilience building, just the common ones I encounter in therapy). These attitudes are not set in stone, so ways to challenge and change them are also presented. It is important to point out that some people, for whatever reason, don't reach out to learn resilience; they are overwhelmed and demoralized by their unsuccessful attempts to cope with adversity or misfortune and happiness continually eludes them. A few will see suicide as the only option to end their suffering: 'Suicide rates among people with spinal cord injuries, for example, are more than seven times greater than among the general population' (Ubel, 2006: 10). Such people require a compassionate understanding of their plight, not condemnation because they fail to overcome the challenges they face. (As I pointed out in Chapter 1, resilience is not about dividing people into winners or losers, quitters or fighters but offered as a capacity open to all to learn.)

'It's not my fault I've been made a victim'

This means feeling helpless in the face of adverse events, continually blaming others for your misfortunes thereby making clear distinctions in your mind between villains and victims, and not taking responsibility for bringing about change in your life. Additionally, you can feel morally superior because of the suffering you have to endure which has been or is being caused by others: 'If you only knew the way I'm treated by my in-laws. I have to put with their nasty behaviour every time they come round. I don't know how I survive each visit.' The victim's story can become the only story in your life, forever ready to relate to others – if they're still listening to you – your tales of suffering and helplessness. If you mix with others who have similar stories to tell, you are likely to become involved in a competition to establish whose suffering is the worst. The longer you justify your victim status, the harder it will become to break free of it and develop other facets of your personality and life.

While you may have been treated unfairly at the hands of others and not received the redress you were seeking, it is still your inescapable responsibility to decide if you want to remain dependent upon your pain in order to attract sympathy or to put boundaries around the pain and escape from the victim trap (Wolin and Wolin,

1993). For example, Peter was bullied by his boss and eventually took sick leave having been worn down by the experience: 'Nobody took my complaints seriously. They just said, "It's a tough environment we work in, you've just got to get on with it".' He left his job but couldn't let go of how he'd been treated by his boss who, he later learned, had been promoted. He saw this promotion as his boss being rewarded for treating him badly. In our sessions, he spent some time venting his understandable anger at his boss's mistreatment of him and the company culture that 'turned a blind eye' to such behaviour. But just as importantly we focused on how his continuing anger and sense of helplessness about correcting this injustice were having corrosive effects on his life; principally, his reluctance to find another job in case the bullying happened again.

I argued for two forms of injustice: first, what his boss did to him and, second, the injustice he would do to himself if he did not pursue his dreams and ambitions, forever blaming the bullying for holding him back in life. He considered the second one, the self-inflicted injustice, as the truly destructive one. He saw the sense in regarding the bullying as a time-limited event (it occurred over a six-month period) that would not adversely affect the rest of his life. I taught him some techniques for standing up to a bullying boss (see Chapter 8). Looking beyond the bullying, he felt he was beginning to regain control over his life.

'I'll never get over it'

The 'it' may be a traumatic event, troubled childhood or any misfortune you believe has robbed you of any future happiness or that has irreparably damaged your life. Or as some clients describe it, 'I'm in pieces'. From this viewpoint, it is reasonable to ask: Can a shattered Humpty-Dumpty ever be put together again? (One of my clients said a resounding 'no' to this question, arguing that what has been broken and then reassembled will always remain structurally weak, so I had to find another metaphor for shattered selves becoming whole again.) Flach (2004) argues that 'falling apart' in the face of significant stress is a normal, even necessary, part of the resilience response as during this period of disruption new ways of reacting to adverse life events can be developed so that the pieces of ourselves can be reassembled in sturdier ways. Our old ways of dealing with things have become obsolete, forcing us to find new ways forward. However, this period of disruption is not without its risks. The pieces can be reassembled successfully or fail to cohere into a meaningful whole that leaves you 'forever more or less destabilized' (Flach, 2004: 13). Going through a period of severe stress can be grasped as a valuable learning experience for both present and future benefit or 'thrown away' because you refuse to accept, for example, that anything good can ever come from anything bad.

I saw a 'burnt out' executive, Roger, who had been overwhelmed by the relentless pressures placed upon him. He felt depressed ('I'm a failure, washed up at 42'), angry ('What were they trying to do, kill me?') and ashamed that he couldn't cope with the pressure ('I'm weak'). He believed his life was in pieces, but I pointed out, when he seemed receptive to the message, that humpty-dumpties can be made whole again. Even though he was intrigued that he could reconfigure the pieces of himself and move his life in a different direction, he was unyielding on the point that he should have been able to handle the pressure and he would be 'stained' with the mark of weakness for the rest of his life. He dropped out of therapy after several sessions and I never saw him again. It's possible that the 'sleeper effect' could have taken hold, i.e. Roger being interested in and acting on the idea of a reconfigured and stronger self at a later date in his life, but this could have been wishful thinking on my part.

Sometimes the process of personal repair can take a long time. In a famous long-term study (from youth to old age) of socially disadvantaged men (one of three groups studied), Professor George Vaillant and his team at Harvard University tracked their progress and came up with some surprising and welcome conclusions. A poor start in life doesn't have to mean that a happy and fulfilling existence cannot be achieved eventually through dogged determination:

> The disadvantaged youth becomes a loving and creative success; the child who 'did not have a chance' turns out to be a happy and healthy adult. We have much to learn from these once-fragmented Humpty Dumpties who ten – or even forty – years later become whole.
>
> (Vaillant, 1993: 284)

If you 'open up' someone's life at a particular point, you might see her struggling unsuccessfully against the odds and this snapshot might lead you to make gloomy predictions about how her life is going to turn out. Revisit her life in several years' time and these predictions may have proved inaccurate. I worked in the National Health Service for 20 years and saw many clients who led chaotic, self-destructive lives. Some died, some seemed forever trapped in a cycle of despair, and some pulled through. If I was a betting man I would have lost a lot of money predicting who would and who wouldn't eventually make it.

'I can't stand it!'

Also called low frustration tolerance (LFT; Ellis, 2001), this attitude refers to your perceived inability to endure frustration (e.g. delaying gratification), boredom, negative feelings, hard work (e.g. tackling your procrastination), inconvenience, setbacks; if something cannot be easily attained you quickly give up. The cognitive core of LFT is: 'I can't stand present pain in order to achieve future gain.' LFT is a key reason why some clients drop out of therapy when the hard work of change begins, i.e. putting into daily practice the CBT insights they've gained in discussions with the therapist. LFT is a deceptive philosophy because it encourages you to think that you're winning by avoiding difficulty whereas your life is actually becoming much harder to manage in the longer term as your unresolved problems pile up and opportunities for self-development are not grasped because they seem like too much hard work.

Helen wanted to learn French but left the course after two sessions as she found it embarrassing having to practise in front of others and realized she wasn't going to become immediately fluent in the language. She had tried to learn Spanish and classical guitar the previous year but gave up for the same reasons. She kept vowing to get fit, seek a new job, find a relationship, make life more exciting, but all to no avail. Ironically, in avoiding the discomfort of change she ended up suffering the discomfort of a dull and unfulfilled life. Which is more unendurable, the discomfort of maintaining the status quo in your life or the discomfort of changing it in order to arrive at a brighter future? To make matters worse, she frequently became angry with herself for giving up too easily ('What's wrong with me? Why can't I stick at things?'). She had a double dose of discomfort – a dull life plus being angry with herself for not persevering with her efforts to change. In therapy with me, she kept demanding instant answers to understand her problems and easy solutions to solve them.

When you make LFT statements such as 'I can't stand it when there's a long queue in the shops', what does 'I can't stand it' actually mean? Will you die as a result of having to put up with frustration or go into psychological meltdown because you have to stick with doing boring tasks? Or you may think that you can't be happy if you have to deal with disagreeable events. In fact, many people actually do stand what they believe they can't stand. The challenge is to find better ways of standing it, namely, choosing to seek out the avoided tasks and situations in order to prove to yourself that frustration is indeed tolerable, nothing terrible will happen to you while you're feeling frustrated and that future gain is worth fighting for. In Helen's case, the challenge was to persevere with her efforts, among other things, to learn French and classical guitar. Frustrations in life are inevitable; disturbing yourself about these frustrations doesn't have to be (Hauck, 1980).

'Why me?'

People often ask this question when they've experienced a traumatic event. The answer is usually implicit in the question: 'It shouldn't have happened to me. I've done nothing to deserve this.' (The word 'should', when used by clients throughout this book, is meant in the imperative sense of what must or must not occur.) This suggests you believe in immunity criteria, i.e. reasons why bad events shouldn't happen to you. Your assumption of a just and fair world can be shattered by the traumatic event (Janoff-Bulman, 1992). For example, John was involved in a multiple car crash and sustained some significant injuries. He was very angry about this happening to him. He kept on insisting that he was a 'very conscientious person', which seemed initially puzzling as to how this virtue was connected to the car crash. However, in teasing out John's sense of logic, it rapidly became clear that being a very conscientious person should have given him an exemption from 'anything horrible in life'. He said, 'I could understand it if I'd been a lazy, work-shy kind of person or someone who's a liar and a cheat, an unpleasant person, but I'm not that kind of person.' His idea of how the universe worked had been 'mocked and destroyed'. He now saw himself as the victim of uncontrollable forces and couldn't see how any constructive meaning could be restored to his life.

'Why me?' introspection is unlikely to yield any useful answers that will help you in your time of distress (this is my experience in working with such clients). For what answers would actually satisfy you? That the world can be cruel and unpredictable? Or you were in the wrong place at the wrong time? Or the driver fell asleep at the wheel when he hit you, but there was no malicious intent in his actions? 'Why me?' is an unanswerable question and to keep on searching for answers that will prove ultimately unsatisfactory prevents you from starting to process the trauma in a constructive way.

A very different perspective might provide an answer. 'Why not me?' This question states an unpalatable truth: that no one is immune from the possibility of experiencing tragedy or misfortune in life. When it happens to you, you can still find some happiness and meaning in life (Warren and Zgourides, 1991), which echoes Viktor Frankl's message from Auschwitz which I discussed in the previous chapter (p. 32). Obviously the timing of such a question is crucial. The therapist is likely to be seen as callous if he asks it before the client has been given the space to explore her reactions to the trauma. When the question is eventually asked, in a sensitive, non-accusatory way, it can take different forms such as: 'Have you ever considered that everyone is likely to experience some tragedy or trauma in their life?'

Mary had been mugged and listed her own immunity criteria, principally, 'Bad things shouldn't happen to good people', but came round to the idea of 'Why not me?' She said she found the idea liberating (unlike John) and began to break free from the restraints of 'Why meism'. However, her new belief was: 'Now that I've had my one [mugging] I'll be safe. It's someone else's turn.' The philosophy of 'Why not me?' also includes the possibility that it could happen again, which Mary had not considered. She was reinstating immunity criteria into her new outlook. We discussed the trap she might be setting for herself and she removed these criteria. Two years later Mary was robbed on the Underground. She said that what stopped her 'from completely disintegrating' was her acceptance that horrible things could happen to her again.

'You can't escape the past'

The past maintains its unshakeable and malign grip on your present behaviour ('It's like being chained forever to what happened earlier in my life'), depriving you of any real happiness. It's not the past itself that maintains this grip but the beliefs you have constructed about these past events which you still believe today. It's the beliefs that are the chains. The past is unalterable; your beliefs about it are not (breaking the chains). For example, Darren found out in his teenage years that he'd been adopted and jumped to the conclusion that he must be defective in some way because his real parents had abandoned him. He still believed this when I saw him 15 years later:

MICHAEL: Before you found out you had been adopted, how did you see yourself?

DARREN: I saw myself as okay, just normal.

MICHAEL: What was life like with your adoptive parents?

DARREN: It was happy. I liked it.

MICHAEL: Why did you think there must be something wrong with *you* when you found out your real parents put you up for adoption?

DARREN: It's obvious. Everybody would think like that if it happened to them.

MICHAEL: Could you explain the obvious to me?

DARREN: Well, if you're a loveable baby then your parents would want to keep you. That makes sense, doesn't it?

MICHAEL: Could you be a loveable baby but still be put up for adoption?

DARREN: I suppose so.

MICHAEL: What reasons might there be for doing that?

DARREN: Well, I know about that. I've discussed that with my adoptive parents. My real parents had lots of problems, some of them psychiatric, and they couldn't really cope with their own lives let alone bring up a child, so they wanted the best for me because they couldn't provide it themselves.

MICHAEL: Presumably you don't find that a satisfactory explanation.

DARREN: No, I don't. What continues to anger me all these years later is that if they really wanted me then they would have found a way to keep me. They just would have found a way. It's as simple as that.

MICHAEL: And because they didn't find a way to keep you, the only answer can be is that you were and remain unloveable. And you're stuck with that view of yourself.

DARREN: That's right. What else am I supposed to think then?

MICHAEL: Well, given what you know about your parents' struggles and their inability to cope with their problems, you expected them to somehow become superhuman, fight to keep you and win. In other words, to be the kind of people you wanted them to be, but they couldn't be other than they were at that time which was to struggle unsuccessfully to overcome their problems.

DARREN: That's true. I never saw it that way. I suppose my parents couldn't be anything else other than they were, though it's hard to get my mind round that.

MICHAEL: Another thing to try and get your mind around is that you keep labelling yourself as 'unloveable' because you were adopted. Being adopted didn't make you unloveable, if you were truly unloveable then how could your adoptive parents love you to bits? Being adopted isn't the problem, maintaining this negative view of yourself is. Every day you can decide to keep it or begin to change it.

DARREN: How do I do that then?

MICHAEL: By what we've been doing today: stepping back from this belief that you're unloveable and starting to examine it critically. It's as if you've been brainwashing yourself for 15 years.

Eventually, Darren was able to see and accept the following points: that he had rejected himself when told he had been adopted and, in consequence, had been perpetuating this self-rejection for 15 years; that the quality of his life with his adoptive parents was probably far better than his real parents could have provided; and that who are his 'real' parents isn't determined biologically, but by the people who provided a loving environment for him to grow up within and who continue to stand by him through thick and thin.

'It shouldn't have happened'

How many times have you said that and coupled it with self-depreciation statements such as 'I'm so stupid'? You were hoping for an alternative and favourable outcome to the one that occurred. For example, you're low on petrol and keep passing petrol stations; you're not prepared to queue in your eagerness to get home after a tiring day at the office. You eventually run out of petrol several miles from home and ask incredulously, 'How could this have happened?' Another example might be that you have no skills or interest in DIY but decide reluctantly, at the urging of your partner, to 'have a go' and end up with a host of problems which require the services of a professional to put right. You shake your head in disbelief at the large fees you have to pay for his services.

As Edelman observes (2006: 74): 'Everything that we say and do, including those things that turn out to have negative consequences, happens because all the factors that were necessary for them to occur were present at the time.' From this perspective, these events should have happened, not shouldn't have happened, based upon your thinking and behaviour at that time in that situation. In the first example, your overriding concern was to get home, not to get petrol. In the second example, a kind of magical thinking took hold which led you to believe you would be able to do a reasonable job, not a badly botched one, without having the slightest skills or interest in DIY. So it's futile to keep telling yourself that 'it shouldn't have happened' (as if this will change the outcome of past events) when all the conditions were in place for it to have happened in the way that it did. Instead, turn your attention to learning from these mistakes in order not to repeat them (e.g. go on a DIY course before attempting any further home improvements).

'I'm a failure'

Such self-devaluation keeps you in a state of demoralized inertia as you act in accordance with your self-image; it's as if you have surrendered to the belief and declared: 'This is how I am and this is how I'll stay.' Even though you probably see both of these statements as unchangeable 'facts', they are actually assumptions that you are making about yourself and your life which are open to challenge and change. For example, if you're a 'genuine' failure as a person then all you can ever do – past, present and future – is fail; even if you wanted to succeed your essence or identity as a 'failure' wouldn't allow it (Dryden, 2001). A review of your life to this point will definitely not support this idea that you're a failure if you're open to finding disconfirming evidence, and your future is still to be revealed.

However, what is likely to stop you from seeing this disconfirming evidence is your negative belief functioning as a self-prejudice (Padesky, 1994), i.e. your 'I'm a failure' belief rejects any evidence that might contradict it and seeks evidence only to confirm it. Think of a belief you don't agree with such as 'All woman are bad drivers'. While listening to the person holding this belief, you might make yourself incensed: 'Why can't he see that women, just like men, are both good and bad drivers? Women have a better safety record than men, they are more careful. He's such a pig-headed git!' He won't be able to hear you because he has a fixed attitude and no amount of contrary evidence is going to shift it (at least not yet). So, if we come back to your view that you're a failure, then you're doing exactly the same thing that he's doing, namely, discounting any evidence that doesn't fit in with your point of view. Some of my clients give this belief-as-self-prejudice a name such as 'ratbag' or 'the whisperer' (e.g. 'That ratbag is talking again but I'm listening to her less and less'). And the reason you're paying less attention is because you're looking at all the evidence about yourself and your life, not just at the care-fully edited 'failure' version.

All self-devaluation beliefs are illogical because they are based on the part–whole error, i.e. an aspect of the self (e.g. a failed relationship) can never capture the complexity of the whole (you) or the totality of your life. There are other aspects of you that also contribute to making up the whole, but these are overlooked in your rush to self-condemnation. For example, when something goes right in your life does this make you a success? Can you be a failure yesterday and a success today? Neither label can do justice to the complexity of a person. Would you attach labels to your children and announce to the world that you've captured their essence as human beings? The inevitable failures and setbacks that you experience are part of the story of your life, but not the whole story.

'Why can't I find happiness?'

This plaintive enquiry is often heard in therapy with clients hoping that the therapist will come up with a happiness formula for them. No matter what the person tries, happiness continues to elude her, so each new activity undertaken (e.g. yoga) is interrogated 'Will *this* make me happy?' On the other hand, the person who achieves the success he has been chasing (e.g. gaining a much sought after position in the company) often experiences post-success disillusion-ment ('I thought this would be the answer to everything') as he believed all his difficulties in life would disappear once his dreams were realized. So he sets himself another goal in his attempt to capture happiness but once again goal achievement doesn't bring happiness in its wake. As Grayling (2002: 71) remarks: 'It has wisely been said that the search for happiness is one of the main sources of unhappiness in the world.'

If the search for happiness does indeed end in unhappiness, then how are we to be happy? Auschwitz survivor Viktor Frankl explained thus: 'Happiness cannot be pursued; it must ensue. One must have a reason to "be happy." Once the reason is found, however, one becomes happy automatically' (1985: 162). What he meant by this is that happiness is a by-product or the result of an interesting and meaningful life (ensue), not the central goal of your life (pursued). For example, I enjoy seeing my son, reading and writing books, taking the dogs for walks, enjoying the company of my friends, running courses, listening to all kinds of music. These things are not done in order to make me happy, but for the intrinsic pleasure I get from these things as they give shape and meaning to my life. I enjoy them for their own sake and, therefore, happiness will be kept in its place as a secondary concern in my life (for the record, I'm reasonably happy). I believe that Frankl's message is an eminently wise one and the 'formula' I teach my clients if they are receptive to it. Some of them say they are now seeking a more meaningful and interesting life, not pursuing happiness, but, alas, are maintaining the old attitude (e.g. 'I've always wanted to do choir singing, so I joined a choir, but it's not making me happy!').

'I shouldn't have to struggle in coping with setbacks'

In Chapter 1 I discussed the false view that resilience is 'bouncing back' from adversity (unless adversity is so loosely defined that missing the bus and deciding to walk the short distance home is seen as 'bouncing back' from hardship). Such a view encourages what might be called resilience perfectionism, i.e. you expect yourself to respond to an adversity in a constructive and effortless way that often elicits the admiration of others. Struggling to recover from misfortune departs from this ideal response and you angrily condemn yourself for failing to act 'in the right way'. Effort and struggle are to be despised as they point to deficiencies of character (Dweck, 2006): 'I take every setback in my stride.

Nothing fazes me. I see people flailing around when things go wrong. Why can't they pull themselves together and get on with it? It's pathetic to watch.'

I once saw a senior manager, nicknamed 'the bulldozer' by his colleagues, who thought that every problem or obstacle could either be 'flattened' or pushed aside until one day at work he experienced a panic attack and discovered that his bulldozing tactics didn't work with this problem. In fact, his panic attacks were getting worse and, in consequence, his performance and concentration were suffering. He was angry and dumbfounded by this state of affairs and kept asking, 'How could this happen to *me*?' He had a fixed view of his character and believed it would function in the way he told it to as if it were an obedient dog. Within the context of personal growth and learning, I explained to him that he could deal with the panic attacks relatively quickly if he allowed me to show him how. His usual response was 'You don't understand. This is not *me*!' His panic attacks undoubtedly belonged to him but, in his mind, they belonged to a weak person; as he never saw himself as weak, therefore they couldn't be part of him. Why couldn't I understand that? He feared his character was beginning to unravel as he couldn't see a solution to a problem that he shouldn't have. After a few sessions, he left therapy none the wiser and berated himself for coming in the first place as this was another worrying sign of the 'weakness' he was forbidden to have.

Needless to say, this is a non-resilient response to dealing with panic attacks because there will come a time when your expected (or in his case fixed) way of responding to adverse events doesn't materialize or isn't fit for purpose any longer and new ways need to be explored if there's going to be a favourable outcome. Your way may have been the right way so far, but it doesn't have to remain the only way.

'I need to know'

Intolerance of uncertainty is the core issue for most people who worry (Leahy, 2006). You believe you have to know now what's going to happen. Not knowing will leave you feeling on edge and you won't be able to focus on anything else. You can't enjoy life with this uncertainty hanging over you and you continually dwell on 'What if?' thoughts (e.g. 'What if she is having affair?'), which generate more 'What ifs?' such as 'What if she leaves me?', 'What if

I can't cope on my own?' and 'What if I can't pay the mortgage?' These ever-proliferating 'What ifs?' lead you to conclude that you have many more problems than you actually have and that you're losing control of your mind. For example, Stanley had been suspended from work pending a disciplinary hearing and brooded endlessly on losing his job, the shame involved in being sacked, finding another job at 45, never being happy again – whatever could go wrong in his life would now go wrong. He kept on insisting in our sessions: 'If they could just tell me today whether they're going to keep me or kick me out, then at least I would be put out of my misery. This disciplinary process is going to go on for another few months. It's mental torture. They should bloody well give me a decision instead of dragging it out!'

The mental torture was largely self-inflicted as Stanley demanded that the disciplinary process run to his timetable, not the company's. He kept on assuming that the outcome of the hearing would mean the loss of his job rather than he might keep it, and that he couldn't focus on anything else in his life until he had a decision. Instead of demanding to know the unknowable before a decision was announced, Stanley focused on what he could know and do, such as re-engaging in daily family activities. Additionally, Stanley flooded himself with uncertainty every day (Leahy, 2006) by saying to himself many times 'I could possibly lose my job'; in order to tolerate this thought without distress, he focused on developing contingency plans in case this did happen (he'd been avoiding doing this), and realized that any shame he may experience would be time limited, not eternal. By undertaking these activities, Stanley felt in control of himself in the face of uncertainty. He did lose his job, but the shock was moderate and he found another one within three months. Learning to tolerate uncertainty can bring forth some unexpected strengths even if the results you were looking for from the situation don't materialize.

'I don't feel confident'

How many times have you said this before trying anything new? Why should you feel confident if you haven't done it before? I see clients with performance anxiety (e.g. running a workshop or engaging in public speaking for the first time) who want to be articulate, witty, insightful, calm and cool, answer every question with impressive authority and get wonderful evaluations from the audience for their performance; in other words, they want to deliver a perfect performance. Yet their fear is falling well below this very high standard and being revealed as hopelessly incompetent, a laughing stock.

They always start in the wrong place in assessing their performance: they're beginners, not accomplished performers, so it's important to have beginner's expectations, not those of a star performer. If they do want to become star performers, then they need to do an apprenticeship in public performing rather than, in their minds, achieving instant acclaim. Feeling confident before you do something new and potentially risky is putting the cart before the horse. Furthermore, courage usually comes before confidence: you're prepared to take the risk of putting yourself in your discomfort zone and staying there without knowing in advance how the situation will turn out. Your legs shake and your knees knock but you force yourself into the limelight. Talk of confidence at this stage is premature. Also, your view of confidence is one-sided as it only envisages a successful outcome. Being resilient means that real confidence embraces both success and defeat – neither is taken too seriously – and that learning from whatever happens is the true focus for self-development.

'I'm a pessimist by nature'

This usually means that when you have a setback you believe the consequences will be catastrophic, wiping out any present or future happiness. You're unlikely to persevere when the going gets tough ('What's the point?') and you slip back into a state of helplessness and self-blame, believing that you have no control over events in your life. Seligman (1991) states that this pessimistic outlook consists of three key elements when a negative event occurs: *permanence* ('It's going to last forever'); *pervasiveness* ('It's going to undermine everything I've tried to achieve in my life'); and *personalization* ('It's my fault'). When my clients say that pessimism is part of them, they usually mean it's inborn and therefore unchangeable. Some clients declare at the beginning of therapy 'You won't be able to help me'. (I see this as a hypothesis to be talked about and tested, not an accurate prediction of how therapy will unfold.) Optimists, by contrast, see negative events as temporary ('It will blow over soon'), specific ('It only affects one area of my life'), and place responsibility for the event on an external cause ('My boss was in a foul mood today'), or take personal responsibility without self-condemnation ('I was rather slow on this occasion in getting the report in on time'). Pessimists dwell on their problems whereas optimists seek constructive ways of dealing with them.

How we explain events to ourselves is called explanatory style and optimists and pessimists, as you can see, have two very different explanatory styles. These two styles are habitual ways of thinking, but habits can be changed. You can learn through sustained effort to become more optimistic in your style of thinking, you can choose a different viewpoint. Martin Seligman, an eminent psychologist and author of *Learned Optimism* (1991), has to battle with his own pessimistic outlook:

> I am not a default optimist. I am a dyed-in-the-wool pessimist; I believe that only pessimists can write sober and sensible books about optimism, and I use the techniques that I wrote about in *Learned Optimism* every day. I take my own medicine, and it works for me.
>
> (Seligman, 2003: 24)

One of the techniques he uses to start changing his pessimistic explanatory style is the ABC model that I discussed in the previous chapter:

A = adversity
B = beliefs
C = consequences – emotional and behavioural

For example, if you fail to get the promotion you were seeking (A) and feel despair and withdraw from others (C) you might believe (B) 'I'm going to be stuck at this level until I retire. My career is ruined. I'm incompetent.' Remember B is the crucial part of this model. You can examine these beliefs using the following criteria I described in Chapter 2.

1   *Are your beliefs rigid or flexible?* 'Rigid. I'm not allowing any other viewpoints into my thinking about this situation including how I see my own performance. My rigid beliefs are preventing me from adjusting to the reality of the current situation.'

2   *Are your beliefs realistic or unrealistic?* 'Unrealistic. There will
    be other opportunities for advancement in the company and
    I still have a career though it's not keeping to the timetable I
    wanted. The company obviously doesn't see it from my point
    of view. If I was truly incompetent I probably wouldn't have a
    career.'
3   *Are your beliefs helpful or unhelpful?* 'They're unhelpful as I
    spend a lot of time brooding about not getting the promotion,
    how unfair it all is, which is affecting my performance at work
    and leading to a bad atmosphere at home.'
4   *Would you teach your beliefs to others?* 'No. They're unreason-
    able. The world of work would be hellish if everyone reacted in
    the way I did to setbacks.'

From such an examination, alternative and reasonably optimistic
beliefs can emerge. You're not likely to have much conviction in
them straightaway as they're unfamiliar and haven't been acted
upon.

> **A = adversity**: not getting the promotion you wanted.
> **B = beliefs**: 'It's highly unlikely I will be stuck at this level until I
> retire as there are no more jobs for life. I can seek further
> advancement in this company or move to another job. Stuck-
> ness is not a fact, but a state of mind. My career has encountered
> a setback, nothing more. I can learn to deal with it instead of
> dwelling on it. I need to remind myself that I can still enjoy my
> job. My competence has been established by the quality of the
> work that I do. My performance appraisals are usually very
> good. I don't suddenly become incompetent because I didn't get
> the promotion. If I was truly incompetent, I would have been
> kicked out long ago.'
> **C = consequences**: emotional – disappointed but hopeful (that
> other opportunities lie ahead); behavioural – re-engage in
> productive activities with your colleagues and family.

Optimistic beliefs are balanced, flexible and realistic and can be
lengthy as you look at the situation in the round, not in the rigid
and extreme way characterized by pessimistic beliefs. Seligman
(1991) made the case for flexible optimism because there might be
specific situations where a pessimistic explanatory style might be
more appropriate than an optimistic one and will help you to avoid

the high risks you're running (e.g. if you've been drinking, assume you will be stopped by the police and take a cab instead; if you're tempted to plagiarize material to put into your college assignment, assume you will be found out by your tutor; and if you lie about your achievements on your CV, assume this will be discovered by your employer).

Undermined, but not forever

In this chapter I have looked at some of the attitudes that undermine resilience building and suggested ways of replacing them with resilience-oriented attitudes. This transition can be slow and difficult and it is easy to give up and fall back into familiar but self-defeating attitudes and behaviours. Considerable change is possible no matter how long you've been stuck in your ways, but the starting point as always is a willingness to be open to new ideas and experiences if you want to start developing a resilient outlook, which is the subject of the next chapter.

Chapter 4

Making yourself more resilient

Introduction

The development of resilience can start at any time for any reason (development means building on what strengths and skills you already have as well as identifying those you lack). You may seek therapy to construct some skills from scratch (e.g. learning to problem solve in a methodical way, see Chapter 5) or because you feel helpless in a particular situation that you believe you should be responding to resiliently (e.g. 'I had my car stolen and I can't stop crying. What's wrong with me?'). Some people assume that their resilience skills will transfer automatically from one situation to another and are stymied when they discover this isn't the case (e.g. being assertive with a rude colleague reduces his ill-tempered behaviour towards you but doesn't work with your new, noisy neighbour who threatens violence when you ask him to turn down his music and you feel powerless in the face of his threats). Or you say you fully understand the importance of thinking and acting flexibly in the face of challenging and changing circumstances – a key resilience quality – yet you absolutely insist that what's happening in this situation shouldn't be happening, a denial of reality (e.g. having to reapply for your job when your company is taken over by a competitor). You threaten to resign over this issue even as you realize how irrationally you're behaving: 'Reapplying for your job is quite commonplace these days. I know that. So why am I getting so hot under the collar about it?' (reapplying for your job may have violated one of your core values such as being treated fairly which means not having to reapply – once is enough!).

Developing resilience can be forced on to you by the sudden death of your beloved partner, having a heart attack at the height of your career or your partner threatening to leave you if you don't seek professional help for your heavy drinking. I say 'can be forced on to you' because you may not derive new meaning and direction in your life from these events or believe that being 'blackmailed' into change can turn out favourably for you (e.g. respectively, you become a recluse as you believe that your life died with your partner, you keep up the punishing work schedule which the cardiologist says will lead to a second, probably fatal, heart attack, and you console yourself with the probability that you can always find another partner instead of stopping drinking to keep this one).

Potential change can be triggered in other ways such as a routine incident (e.g. being stuck for hours in a traffic jam leads you to reflect on the dullness of your life and you decide some major changes are needed); or a dramatic one (e.g. the train you missed crashes, scores of people are injured and several are dead, and the shock of what might have happened to you leads you to ponder if you are making the most of your life when it can be extinguished so suddenly). Boredom may propel you into action or an event may act as an epiphany (revelation) in your life. For example, Hugh was with his friends in the pub one evening when one of them made a joke and he started laughing: 'Suddenly, I seemed to detach from myself as if I was looking down on myself and I thought, "Why are you laughing when you don't find the joke remotely funny?" After that, I was quiet for most of the evening and walked home alone. I realized how much of a people pleaser I was and I didn't like myself for that, but I was determined to change even if I didn't know how to do it at that stage.'

These turning points – and they can only be seen as such in hindsight once change is well under way or achieved – usually crystallize your thinking rather than offering you a perspective you've never considered before. (Hugh had been troubled by his people-pleasing behaviour but reluctantly accepted it as necessary if he wanted to be 'part of the group'.) Whatever the reason you have for initiating change in your life, persevering with it in order to achieve your goals is another key resilience strength. Unfortunately, the initial surge in change activities can quickly die away and your life returns to business as usual which last week or month you were fed up with.

Looking for your strengths

I mentioned in Chapter 1 that most people do display resilient behaviour in their lives, but some may not be aware of this because they think resilience is bouncing back from terrible adversity and haven't experienced these kinds of incidents or they only have vague ideas of what resilience is. So looking for your strengths is an important starting point in understanding resilience. Some writers (e.g. Reivich and Shatté, 2003) have resilience quotient (RQ) tests in their books in order to determine your current RQ level. These tests are based on the factors or abilities they believe constitute resilience. I don't give RQ tests but I do ask my clients how they've dealt successfully with previous problems or what qualities they like about themselves in order to uncover the strengths that can be used to tackle their present concerns (usually clients can quickly describe their weaknesses but often struggle to list their strengths and qualities).

Rachel, who was 27, thought she was 'falling behind' when she compared her post-university progress to that of her friends who left university at the same time as she did. Her presenting problem was her inability, when criticized at work, to separate the criticism of her specific behaviour from criticism of herself: 'I immediately rush to defend myself. I feel crushed and hurt and don't pay attention to whether the criticism might be justified. I know it's a weakness and I want to stop reacting like that but I can't seem to stop myself doing it.' When we looked for strengths in her life she was initially puzzled because she equated strengths with making the same kind of progress as her friends in terms of career advancement and higher salary. On further examination she revealed that she:

- runs marathons
- has not had a day off work
- completed her degree
- finishes tasks she is given
- believes that problems do have solutions
- keeps her word
- has friends she sticks by and who stick by her
- worked hard to pay off debts incurred at university
- is generally optimistic.

RACHEL: I didn't think about those things. I think I know what you're trying to do but I'm not quite sure.

MICHAEL: What does running marathons suggest about you?

RACHEL: That I've got determination, stamina, and I like doing them. I started at university when I joined the running club. I was overweight and unfit and wanted to do something about it. I really enjoy them now.

MICHAEL: You say you haven't had a day off work.

RACHEL: That's right.

MICHAEL: Why don't you take a day off like some people do when they're not genuinely ill?

RACHEL: I thought about it but it just doesn't seem right to pretend that you're ill when you're not.

MICHAEL: Are you tempted to take a day or two off when you feel under pressure from the criticism?

RACHEL: Tempted to, but I don't want to run away from it. I want to deal with it.

MICHAEL: You've paid off your debts from university.

RACHEL: I didn't want those hanging over my head.

MICHAEL: Okay. I won't go through the whole list with you, but what do you think I'm getting at?

RACHEL: That I've got some pretty good qualities and can accomplish things when I put my mind to it but I'm struggling with this issue.

MICHAEL: Struggle doesn't seem to be something you're afraid of. Given what you know about yourself, what do you predict the outcome will be with this issue?

RACHEL: That there will be a solution to it and I'll find it with your help.

MICHAEL: And I would suggest we are already halfway there without even getting into the detailed specifics of this issue yet because of the strengths you already have.

RACHEL: Why aren't I coping then with this issue if I have all these strengths and good qualities?

MICHAEL: Because each new challenge or problem that we face may reveal what skills and abilities we lack to deal with it. At that point we have a choice: to learn these skills, retreat from the problem hoping it will go away or just give up.

RACHEL: I want to learn to deal with it, not give up or retreat.

MICHAEL: And that's why we're already halfway there to a solution.

Rachel learnt to focus on dealing with criticisms of her specific behaviours (e.g. her boss accused her of 'falling down on the job' when she failed to respond immediately to an urgent email from him) without turning these specific criticisms into condemnation of her overall performance at work ('I'm incompetent'): 'Some of these criticisms are definitely valid which I'm putting right. Feeling sorry for myself just drained the energy away from problem solving.' Additionally, as she compared herself unfavourably with the progress her friends were making in their careers, she was prone to see herself as a failure for not keeping pace with them. She now decided to evaluate her career progress based on her own values, desires and timetable and stopped looking through the lens of her friends' progress to do this for her.

Examining daily life for evidence of your resilience

Strengths can be found in the daily activities you undertake yet probably dismiss as 'just getting on with it' and do not see this as evidence of resilience in action (Padesky, 2008). For example, you take the children to and from school every day, look after your pets, keep the house tidy, make sure the fridge is full, keep your dental and GP appointments, pay the bills on time, look after your children when they're ill even if you're ill yourself, and so on. You might see your behaviour as on automatic pilot as you breeze through the day ticking off all the things you've done. Believe it or not, your behaviour shows dedication, perseverance, self-discipline and problem solving. Now imagine you wake up tomorrow and decide it's too much effort to take your children to school on time, the dogs out for a walk, go shopping or keep appointments. The cracks in the structure of your life would begin to show pretty quickly, and if you persisted in this 'not bothering' approach you would not be the only one to suffer. That this unravelling of your life does not occur is attributable to the routine resilience you display every day.

Revisiting past adversities to uncover useful lessons to help you cope better with current events

Another way to uncover strengths is to go back to past adversities and think again about how well or badly you faced them. You might say that you coped badly in these situations because you did not immediately rise to the challenge and deal with them quickly and effectively or display some other ideal response. For example, when Bill found out that his 19-year-old son was using heroin he went 'ballistic' and read the riot act to him: 'Essentially, it was stop using or I'll kick you out of the house.' He also felt guilty ('I must have failed my son in some way because he has become a heroin addict') and was fearful that his son would end up in the gutter or worse. He thought that shouting at his son and ordering him to get off heroin would do the trick, but all to no avail. Bill took his son to see drug specialists who put him on methadone programmes (to wean him off street heroin) and arranged for him to go into rehabilitation centres, but he usually left them after a few days and returned to drug use. Bill thought he was a failure as a father because he wasn't able to get his son to kick the drugs for good. He should have the ability to make his son stop (this viewpoint assumes that he is all-powerful and can make his son do what he commands).

Looking back at those times, Bill now realizes that he did the best he could, though it took him some time to see this: 'I didn't realize how little influence I would have over my son compared to the drugs. They were everything to him. The drug specialists told me that heroin addiction was a chronically relapsing condition. I should prepare myself for the long haul. He lied to me a lot which was very upsetting but I eventually realized he couldn't distinguish between truth and lies any longer. He stole money from us, shoplifted, did petty thievery to get money for the drugs. He went to prison for a short while. He kept on saying that he had reached rock bottom and the only way now was up. Initially, this would fill me with hope, but then I quickly realized there was always another rock bottom beneath the current rock bottom.

The best piece of advice the drug people gave me was to not neglect my other children as I would probably experience problems with them if I did, and to get on with my life as best as I could. I joined a parents' support group which helped me a lot to gain more understanding of how to cope better. I was able to forgive my son for all the pain and grief he had caused the family as he was in the grip of this addiction. This was another way of coming to terms with the situation. I learned to support my son in a positive way if he wanted to make another attempt to give up the drugs – definitely not give him money to pay off his drug debts – but to give up the idea that I could get him to stop. That was my son's responsibility to do, whenever that would be. I eventually lost touch with him. So I don't know where he is or how he is today and, of course, I still miss him. The most powerful lesson I learnt from those times was to accept my limitations as a parent without despair and focus on what I could influence – my own life and those of my other children if they were prepared to listen to me. But it took some time for that lesson to sink in, but that lesson keeps me in good stead whenever I face a new problem: step back and have a good look to see what's in my control. For example, my daughter is getting married again. I think the man she's going to marry is totally wrong for her, I certainly don't like him. I've said my piece to her about this subject and I'm not going any further than that or get myself upset over it. It's her life and she'll have to get on with it.'

Envisaging future adversities to build additional resilience strengths

In Chapter 3, in the section 'I need to know' (pp. 49–50), I discussed the kind of 'What if?' worrying thinking that generates more problems because potential solutions are not being sought to challenge the ever-increasing number of 'What if?' questions. However, 'What if?' thinking can play a constructive role when used in contingency planning:

> A unique feature of resilience is that you can promote the factors [of resilience] independently of experiences of adversity. You can even engage in a game of 'what if?' This means you can pretend an adversity or tragedy has occurred, and you can imagine what you would do to deal with it and which resilience factors you would use.
>
> (Grotberg, 2003: 13)

In your imagination, you can begin to work through dealing with this future adversity and list the stuck points you encounter along the way. It is important that the future adversity is an actual concern (e.g. your partner leaving you) and not one that is highly improbable but interesting to speculate about (e.g. living on the streets). For example, Sophie was a very experienced workshop presenter and had faced tough audiences which she handled with aplomb. She was resourceful, self-confident, had a sense of humour, possessed good interpersonal skills, was not afraid to take risks and had persevered to build up her own successful business. However, when she thought about being laughed at when presenting a workshop, she mentally disintegrated. 'Why can't I get a handle on this blasted issue?' She had tried to imagine them laughing with her instead of at her, carrying on with the presentation and pretending not to hear the laughter, looking at the group sternly to stop the laughter abruptly, engaging in self-deprecating humour to lessen the harsh impact of the laughter, lecturing them on the insensitivity of their laughter, but each tactic she considered never really convinced her that it would work. What I wanted to know to start off the investigation was:

MICHAEL: What is the meaning you attach to being laughed at?
SOPHIE: Well, I don't like it.
MICHAEL: I understand that but this fear strikes deep into your heart which suggests it's more profound than simply not liking it.
SOPHIE: I'm not really sure. I know it's something I dread even though I have bags of confidence and should be able to deal with it.
MICHAEL: But presently you can't seem to. Try to imagine as vividly as possible an audience laughing at you. What might have you done to trigger the laughter?
SOPHIE: Tripped over or done something like that, really stupid.
MICHAEL: How are you feeling?
SOPHIE: Angry, but really feeling humiliated, powerless.
MICHAEL: And you're humiliated and powerless because . . .?
SOPHIE: My credibility has been destroyed through my stupidity, everything I've worked damn hard for is gone and there's nothing I can do about it. I know it's ridiculous, but there it is.

Sophie regarded herself as a very optimistic person but was shocked at how quickly she allowed herself, if laughed at, to become engulfed by the pessimistic explanatory style I discussed in Chapter 3 (pp. 51–54): *permanence* ('My credibility has been destroyed'); *pervasiveness* ('Everything I've worked damn hard for is gone'); and *personalization* ('My stupidity'). She said she went from 'confidence to collapse in the blink of an eye'. Being laughed at also had distant echoes ('I felt the same way in school when people laughed at me'). The most important step was to change the meaning of being laughed at – to extract the 'poison' from the laughter and thereby make it harmless which would stop Sophie feeling helpless. Sophie saw herself as 'being put down' by the laughter (she had felt the same at school) and therefore her professional credibility wasn't being taken seriously. She felt angry towards the audience for their behaviour ('How dare you bastards laugh at me!'). So this is how she tackled the issue:

- By accepting that there is no reason why she can't be laughed at no matter how seriously she takes herself in that situation – she doesn't have the power to stop people doing it.
- By acknowledging that it would have to take something pretty spectacular to destroy her professional credibility, not just tripping over or dropping a bunch of papers.
- By understanding that the real problem was her evaluation of what the laughter means, not the laughter itself – only she can put herself down, not the laughter.
- Thereby re-evaluating being laughed at as something to put up with, not to be used to put herself down with: 'I remain highly professional even though I might have done something silly or made a mistake.'

Sophie practised this new outlook in imagery for a couple of weeks: imagining powerfully and vividly dropping some papers on the floor (or other worrying incidents), being laughed at but feeling in control of herself as she had removed the 'poison' from the laughter, and saw herself bending down to pick up the papers by which time the laughter had subsided. Instead of waiting for this future adversity to happen, she wanted to bring it into the present in order to practise self-management. Therefore, her next step was to try out her new approach in a forthcoming presentation. She accidentally on purpose knocked over a plastic cup of water while talking to a group of managers. She was pleased with her ability to keep on talking to the group while clearing up the mess and was surprised that there wasn't more laughter. A few members of the audience came forward to help her. She had never considered that some people might help her rather than laugh at her. Through these methods she regained the sense of perspective – the optimistic explanatory style – she usually displayed in other difficult situations: that the incident was temporary (lasting a couple of minutes at most), limited to this specific area (the part of the workshop where she knocked over the cup of water) and took immediate responsibility to clear up the mess without putting herself down or feeling angry towards the audience and thereby replacing her catastrophic view with a realistic assessment of what actually happened.

Dealing with adversity as it unfolds

You can learn from past adversities and anticipate what you might do to deal with future ones, but what do you do when you're unexpectedly faced with adversity? Grotberg (2003: 20) observes that 'a major problem of living through adversity is that it begins to have a life of its own . . . you [are] increasingly reacting to what is happening rather than being proactive'. She states that it's important for you to try and exert some control over what is happening to you by monitoring how you are responding to the adversity and its aftermath and making adjustments in your responding as events unfold, e.g. stop allowing well-meaning others to do too much for you as this will help to reduce your current sense of helplessness, or instead of trying to suppress your feelings, begin expressing them to sympathetic others in order to challenge the idea that you're all alone in the world and no one will be able to understand what you're going through. This ability to exert some control over adverse events will help you to find a path out of your present predicament.

In Chapter 2 I mentioned that I had a lumbar disc prolapse in 1997. My back was giving me some trouble a few weeks before that Sunday evening when I bent down to pick something up and it 'went'. I ended up lying on the floor, breathing rapidly, my left side in seemingly perpetual painful spasm. When I was lying on the floor I accepted immediately that something pretty substantial had happened to my back without feeling sorry for myself (this is not a retrospectively and heroically embellished account of what happened, but what I was thinking and doing at the time). I dragged myself over to the telephone and called for an ambulance. While waiting for it to arrive, I slowed down my rapid breathing as best I could. Even though I appeared to be in a helpless position I was, in fact, taking control of what I was able to, namely, choose what attitude I wanted to adopt in this situation. While lying on a trolley in casualty, I pledged myself to follow whatever advice the professionals decreed was the quickest way to get back on my feet. After being given painkillers and tranquillizers as well as a letter for my GP, I took a taxi home and lay down on the bed.

The acute phase of the adversity was over; now the rehabilitation phase after a few more investigations (e.g. MRI scan) had been carried out. I was eager for this phase to start so I could build myself up again, but within the limitations imposed by the prolapse, and get back to work which I was able to do within several weeks. I wanted to avoid the kind of thinking I had seen some of my clients display with regard to their own pain and physical impairments such as: 'I have to stop doing tasks when I'm in pain [as opposed to learning to tolerate some pain while carrying out these tasks]'; 'My body keeps letting me down [it will if you keep insisting on having exactly the same body you did before the accident]'; or 'I'm powerless to do anything with my life [powerless is a hypothesis, not a fact, and you might be surprised to learn that you have more power than you realize if you're prepared to experiment with new ways of doing things that are within your current limitations].'

These beliefs prevent you from seeing any brighter future beyond the pain and increase both your psychological distress and the intensity of the physical pain. I didn't want to go down that road and therefore I was always monitoring myself to ensure that I focused on what I could do to hasten my recovery such as going swimming and getting an exercise bike and accepting (without liking it) that lifelong management of my back pain was now called for (e.g. doing back exercises twice a day to keep it flexible, regular visits to the chiropractor) including periods when the pain flares up again and my mobility is restricted. In this way, adversity is faced, managed and kept in its proper place so it doesn't overshadow everything else in my life.

Andrew was walking home from the railway station one night when he was attacked in an alleyway: 'There were two of them. It all happened so fast, it was over in seconds. They punched and kicked me and I fell to the ground. They took my wallet, watch and mobile phone. I got myself up and staggered home. All I could think of was to cancel my credit cards as I had these images of my money flowing out of my bank account as these two bastards went on an immediate spending spree. That was my only concern at the time. When I got home my wife became distressed when she saw my cuts and bruises, my nose was bleeding. In fact, I had to calm her down before I could get to the phone to cancel the cards. Once that was done I felt relieved. My wife wanted to rush me to casualty but I couldn't be bothered to sit there for hours waiting to be seen. So I patched myself up as best as I could and saw my GP the next day. I didn't see what happened to me as any major trauma – my father went through far, far worse in the war – but my wife and some of my friends kept on insisting I was probably traumatized and didn't realize it or was denying it, so mainly to placate my wife I came to see you.'

I saw Andrew for one session. I certainly did not want to pathologize (i.e. turn into a problem) his resilient response to the attack. In fact, he showed remarkable resilient qualities. As soon as the attack was over he employed an immediate problem-solving focus (cancel the credit cards). He showed empathy in attending to his wife's distress while he was bruised and bleeding as well as coming to therapy for her sake. In our conversation there was no 'Why me?' anguish (he shrewdly observed that such anguish would be self-generated and he didn't want to add that to the physical aches and pains he was experiencing from the attack). He refused to let the attack dominate his life and his only concession to it was to avoid walking through the alleyway at night. Also, he got bored with being asked 'How have you been feeling since the attack? It must have been terrible.' He said he hadn't lost his sense of humour, so his usual reply to this question was: 'What's really terrible is to keep on being asked about the attack. How about asking me about my garden instead?'

Move out of your comfort zone in order to develop greater tolerance for experiencing discomfort

As I mentioned in the lengthy definition of resilience in Chapter 1, dealing with the challenges of daily living helps to prepare you for the inevitable adversities that lie ahead. How so? By tackling the activities you've been avoiding, you raise your threshold, sometimes significantly, for dealing with frustrations and tolerating distress and discomfort. This 'discomfort practice' helps to change your view of yourself as more capable and stronger than you imagined. As Irvine (2009: 112) points out:

> By undertaking acts of voluntary discomfort . . . we harden ourselves against misfortunes that might befall us in the future. If all we know is comfort, we might be traumatized when we are forced to experience pain or discomfort, as we someday

almost surely will. [Also] a person who periodically experiences minor discomforts will grow confident that he can withstand major discomforts as well, so the prospect of experiencing such discomforts at some future time will not, at present, be a source of anxiety for him.

For example, for a long time Roger had been avoiding clearing out all the junk that had piled up in the garage, the garden was over-grown, his office at work was untidy – Roger said he just 'couldn't be bothered' with anything that was boring or burdensome. Yet he realized things had to change. 'I need a rocket up my backside to get me moving', so he decided it was time to 'be bothered'.

He started where it was easiest – clearing up his office – but once cleared he had to be consciously aware of every move he made (like driving on the 'wrong' side of the road in Europe) not to clutter it up again and put things away tidily. Next he focused on the garage. He stayed in there each time for at least a couple of hours to ensure that he worked through his disturbed thoughts and feelings ('I hate this boring crap!'). He said he did a lot of swearing and kicking cans around while sorting through which 'crap' to take to the council tip. Then he turned his attention to the garden with a similar stay-at-it attitude. These and other tasks he tackled helped him to see that 'being bothered' increased his sense of self-efficacy, i.e. he could accomplish what he set out to do: 'I don't like them [boring tasks] but I can do them.' His wife had for a long time wanted to move to a new area, but on every occasion she discussed it Roger refused to move, saying he was happy where he was. The real reason, he later admitted, was the huge upheaval it would cause in his life and he didn't want to experience it. This time, however, he agreed and what could have been a major source of stress (as rated on life events questionnaires) went relatively smoothly given his new 'be bothered' outlook.

While Roger avoided boring tasks, Nancy avoided interpersonal conflict whenever possible. She didn't like having to experience 'bad atmospheres' or people thinking ill of her. If she couldn't escape from conflict she felt overwhelmed with anxiety, became tongue-tied and tried to placate the other person by quickly admitting she was in the wrong or apologizing profusely. Nancy's motto was 'anything for a quiet life' but internally she led an unquiet life as she was deeply critical of her passivity and cowardice ('Why can't I stand up for myself?'). As with Roger, Nancy had to embrace what she feared or disliked if she was going to make progress, deliberately seeking discomfort in order to learn how to tolerate it. So she constructed a hierarchy of situations to move through from least to most threatening in terms of confrontation, starting with asking the two boys next door to stop kicking their ball into her garden and putting up with the withering looks from the boys' mother. Other situations she faced included complaining in restaurants about her meal, persistently asking her husband to put his dirty clothes into the washing basket instead of dropping them on the floor, and insisting that a work colleague stop speaking to her in a patronizing way.

The situation she feared the most was saying 'no' to her sister who expected Nancy to do her bidding and became angry if she demurred: 'She treats me like a slave.' 'Correction,' I said. 'You allow her to treat you like a slave. When will the slave rise up and break the chains she has placed on herself because of her quest for the quiet life?' The revolt soon began and her sister stopped speaking to Nancy for a while. Eventually, the relationship was reestablished through Nancy's desire still to see her sister but now under very different conditions. It's important to point out that Nancy's progress was not easy. She was anxious a lot of the time, often feeling physically sick, as she worked her way through the hierarchy and many times considered giving up. The reason she didn't was 'because staying the same was more frightening to me than what I'd have to do trying to be a different person'.

At the end of therapy, Nancy said she had been through an emotional ordeal but felt she had emerged from it a stronger person. At a six-month follow-up appointment, she said her marriage was under severe strain as her husband was considering leaving her as he didn't like the 'new' Nancy and having to change his behaviour in the light of her changes. She wasn't happy about the possible end of her marriage but realized that her husband had taken her for granted for many years and had never encouraged her to be stronger: 'Maybe it's for the best. He wants the old Nancy and I want someone who's going to support me in what I'm now doing. If he does leave, I'm more than ready to cope with living alone. I was already living alone in many ways.'

Like a lot of clients I see, Nancy asked, 'Why didn't I do this much sooner in my life or see it for myself?' My answer is that earlier in your life you were not thinking or acting in ways that would have brought about your current changes. In Nancy's case, thinking 'anything for a quiet life' and avoiding interpersonal conflict were key cognitive and behavioural processes maintaining her problems. What you did at the time is determined by what you were thinking at the time (looking back, it's pointless to insist that you should have been thinking something different). Flowing from this understanding, other points logically slot into place:

- Even if you knew what to do at the time to deal with your problem, you didn't do it.
- Even if you knew what to do and began doing it, you didn't persist with it.
- Even if you considered seeking professional help because you realized you couldn't do it alone, you didn't follow up on this idea.

Therefore, all the conditions were in place in your life to prevent you from dealing effectively with your problems. However, some clients continue trying to challenge this unassailable truth by searching for the 'real' answer or keep torturing themselves with their retrospective and accusatory 'I should have knowns'. Better to enjoy the changes you have made and consider how to build on them in order to get more of what you want from life than remain stuck in a state of irritated puzzlement wondering why you didn't do these things earlier. This state is likely to hold you back from taking full advantage of the changes you've worked so hard to bring about.

Building a strength from scratch

While you may have a range of qualities that you appreciate about yourself, you're still irritated by a particular response that you can't seem to do anything about, no matter what you try. For example, Jonathan described himself as 'oversensitive' to criticism, quick to take offence even if no offence was intended: 'I remember at a meeting a colleague asked me to pass along a jug of water and I immediately reacted to his request by thinking, "He's treating me like a dogsbody, he doesn't have any respect for me. Why didn't he ask someone else or reach over to get it himself?" It was utterly ridiculous to think like that as I was closest to the water. Do you see what I mean? I'm a lost cause.' Also, he was embarrassed that some of his colleagues would preface their comments by saying, 'Now Jonathan, I'm not trying to get at you. I just want to point out . . .'. Jonathan didn't like being treated with kid gloves yet he acted in ways that elicited such behaviour from others (two of his colleagues, however, spoke their minds as they were fed up with the tiptoeing strategy others used around him).

What made Jonathan so sensitive to criticism – real, implied or imagined? He said he wasn't sure as he had been like that for a long time: 'My mind seems to be on the lookout for put-downs.' He said he probably did see himself, at times, as inferior to others, 'My self-esteem can get shaky', but thought he was good at his job and proud of the expertise that others drew upon to complete their projects. As I discussed in Chapter 2, how to overcome a problem is more important than knowing why it exists in the first place, so the focus was on 'toughening up' Jonathan, not seeking answers by extensive trawling through his past.

An ingrained response can be difficult to shift, so a firm commitment to the hard work of change was required which Jonathan agreed to. Then we discussed the important point that you can't be offended without your consent (but you can be harmed without your consent such as being punched in the face), 'You're stupid for not knowing the answer to that easy question'. The person delivering the insult cannot put it into your head unless you 'open the gate' to let it in and the usual reason you do that is because you agree with the insult. If you argue that you wouldn't agree with the insult but would still be offended by it, this is likely to occur because your personal rule that you shouldn't be insulted has been violated, thereby activating your anger, so you still believe you have been offended through rule violation. Insults can't harm you, only offend you if you let them. When Jonathan grasped and agreed with this distinction, the next step was to investigate what options he had when responding to an insult or criticism. He came up with the following:

1   There is no reason why he can't be criticized or insulted (the world does not revolve around his wishes and wants) and it's not the job of others to protect his shaky self-esteem. It's his responsibility to learn how to make it sturdy rather than keep it shaky.
2   Acknowledge the current shortcomings in his performance and develop an action plan to address them.

3   Decide which part of an insult or criticism may be valid and state what he intends to do about it, but point out it could have been said in a friendlier or constructive way.
4   Allow others the right to be wrong about him when he believes their criticisms are unfounded, and also allow himself the right to be wrong about others' behaviour and apologize to them if necessary.
5   Spend as little time as possible with those who are overly critical or ceaselessly fault finding.
6   Seek constructive feedback from those who can help to improve his performance.

In the session, we practised dealing with the insults Jonathan was most sensitive to. With his permission, I 'insulted' him and then he practised his response:

MICHAEL: You're hopeless at bringing meetings to a close at the agreed time.
JONATHAN: Most of my meetings do overrun but not all of them. I don't agree I'm hopeless because that indicates I'll never change which is certainly not my view. [Coming out of the role play] You know when you said 'hopeless' that really struck home.
MICHAEL: Because . . .?
JONATHAN: Because I thought, 'You're right, I am'.
MICHAEL: Someone else starts giving you a verbal kicking, then you take over. I think your self-esteem remains shaky because you are a harsh self-critic. If you move from condemning yourself to compassionately helping yourself to make those changes that you want, then you might see a sturdier self emerging.
JONATHAN: Well, I'm going to keep on practising till I get the hang of what you just said.

Which is what he did. By working intrapersonally (i.e. developing self-supporting beliefs such as 'My performance sometimes is poor but my intrinsic worth as a person stays constant') and interpersonally (i.e. deciding whether to respond to actual insults from his colleagues who, in reality, were the two he never got on with anyway) he experienced his oversensitivity becoming blunted 'as my skin thickened'. Imagined slights or insults fell away sharply. As I discussed in Chapter 1, acting resiliently can be seen as a ratio between helpful and unhelpful behaviour in pursuit of your goal, so it's important that your resilience balance sheet shows more assets (occurrences of helpful behaviour) than liabilities (occurrences of unhelpful behaviour). In Jonathan's case, 70 per cent of the time he was able to respond constructively to criticism while 30 per cent of the time he turned the criticism inwards and 'condemned myself instead of focusing on my behaviour'. At the end of therapy he was working towards his ideal goal: 'The best defense lies in refusing to take offense. The worst defense lies in seeking to be offended at every turn. As Eleanor Roosevelt said, "No one can make you feel inferior without your consent"' (Marinoff, 2004: 99).

Physical fitness doesn't necessarily make you mentally tough

Exercise is good for both physical and mental health. Physically, it helps to reduce your weight and improves your pulse rate, blood pressure and lung capacity (Oyebode, 2007). Mentally, it can lift your mood, reduce stress levels, make you more alert and improve your self-image (you see yourself as more capable and confident because you feel fitter and stronger). Sometimes you can put too much emphasis on getting physically fit and strong as you think this will automatically make you mentally tough and able to deal with anything that comes your way.

Patricia was a compulsive gym goer (a 'gym rat' she called herself). She had a high-pressured job and believed that being fit and slim helped her to cope with this pressure; she looked down on those of her colleagues who were overweight and unfit. Going to the gym for a vigorous workout gave her a tremendous feeling of self-confidence and control over her life: 'I can take on the world.' However, cracks began to show in her high self-confidence if she was unable to get to the gym because of the demands of her job. She became agitated, imagining she was putting on weight and becoming unfit and that her sense of self-control was being eroded (this was based on one day's absence from the gym!). During a period of illness she became frantic with worry that because she couldn't get to the gym or train she was becoming what she despised in others, fat and unfit, and was alarmed by how quickly her tough mindedness was turning into crumble mindedness.

This psychological fragility proved to be the turning point for Patricia; it showed how narrowly based was her sense of identity and control. She started developing a broader range of interests and strengths that she could draw upon at times of difficulty to help her cope better. Also, widening her perspective helped her to see that her identity was composed of a variety of aspects of varying importance, but not to make any of these aspects all-important as this would again 'imprison' her identity. She stopped going to the gym so often (three times a week versus seven days a week) and expanded her constricted life by engaging in more social activities including finding a partner (she hadn't had one for several years). I encouraged her to conduct a survey among the 'despised' group of overweight/unfit colleagues for their views on what constitutes being in control of one's life. The main finding from her survey was having a work–life balance and enjoying both (which opened her eyes to the fact that people can be happy without being fit and slim – this is not everyone's priority in life). In retrospect, she felt her life had been out of balance: either at work or in the gym with little real excitement in between.

Resolve to be more resilient

Virtually everyone has some resilience strengths. This point can be easily forgotten when you're entangled in your present problems and can't see a way forward. This chapter has looked at bringing these overlooked strengths to your attention, learning from past adversities in order to inform your present behaviour when new difficulties emerge, anticipating future adversities to see what additional resilience responses might be needed to deal with them, dealing with adversity as it unfolds and trying to keep some control over what is happening to you, facing what you've been avoiding in order to increase your threshold for tolerating discomfort, and building a strength from scratch to increase your repertoire of problem-solving options. All these things can help to make you more resilient in the face of present and future problems. In this and previous chapters I've discussed some of the strengths that underpin resilience. In the next chapter, I look at the full range of strengths that I believe form a resilient outlook.

Chapter 5

Strengths underpinning resilience

Introduction

How did I arrive at my list of strengths? Through extensive reading of the resilience literature, the valuable learning I've acquired over the years from my clients' struggles with adversity including those who didn't make it, what I've learnt from my training in and practice of cognitive behavioural therapy (CBT) over the last 20 years, my own battles with tough times which helped me to practise what I teach – though certainly not with perfect consistency – and gain deeper insight into the nature of resilience. I'm not claiming to have captured the essence of resilience in these strengths because, as I said in Chapter 1, this essence remains ultimately elusive. But I do believe that if you acquire some or most of these strengths, and add them to your existing ones, this will considerably increase your resilience staying power for facing and overcoming misfortune. Probably all writers on resilience (or, more accurately, the writers I've read) list the attributes, attitudes, qualities, factors, abilities, skills, strengths – whatever term they use – that they believe are the foundation of a resilient outlook. So here is my non-definitive list of the strengths underpinning resilience in no order of importance (even if some entries are considerably longer than others).

From strength to strength

High frustration tolerance (HFT)

This is the ability to endure in times of distress or upheaval without continually complaining how difficult the struggle is or lapsing into self-pity every time a new setback is encountered. Discomfort is to be expected and embraced now in order to suffer less in the future as your problems start to be resolved through the effort you've applied to tackle them. Suffering endlessly and needlessly usually occurs because you won't grasp the nettle of what needs to be done in order to reduce it. Ironically, while avoiding the suffering involved in, for example, ending a relationship that's run its course for you ('She'll feel destroyed and betrayed if I leave her and I'll feel guilty about abandoning her'), you continue to suffer by staying in a relationship that you now hate. This demonstrates that you do have HFT of the kind which, unfortunately, will perpetuate your suffering: 'Every day I stay in this relationship that I want to run away from, I'm proving to myself that I can in fact stand being here, stand being so unhappy because I'm doing nothing about leaving.'

HFT is not emotional masochism, i.e. the higher the level of distress, the greater the sense of endurance and accomplishment: 'I can take the pain!' Too high a level of distress will stop or distract you from achieving your goals, so help from others to reduce this distress might be part of your goal-directed striving. The cognitive core of HFT is 'I can tolerate discomfort and frustration in order to reach my goals' – persistence with purpose. I don't ask my clients if they feel comfortable about what they're going to do as this seems a counterproductive question. You don't develop resilience by staying in your comfort zone, and a continual emphasis on feeling comfortable will not only hamper my clients' progress but also suggest that there is, after all, a way to change painlessly and easily (which some clients are hoping for). Much more productive I find is to discuss with my clients the benefits of acquiring HFT in order to guide themselves through the ups and downs of the change process.

I would suggest that achieving a goal is often less important than what the struggle to achieve it has revealed about you in uncovering strengths that you didn't think you had or seeing yourself in new and sometimes surprising ways. For example, a client who saw herself as 'stupid' for leaving school with minimal academic qualifications entered higher education in her late forties hoping to get a degree yet fearful that her stupidity would be exposed: 'I discovered late in life that I had a love of learning and I wanted to pursue it. The desire was becoming overpowering, so I applied.' She worried about being the oldest in the class (she was) and being ignored or laughed at by the younger students (she wasn't), or being ridiculed by the tutors and students when she gave her views or asked questions (this didn't happen). While she was overjoyed at getting her degree, the real satisfaction was witnessing the transformation of herself from 'supposed thicko to something of an intellectual': 'I was having a coffee in the bar, surrounded by lots of students chattering away, and I felt immensely happy. I was one of them, I'd made it. I completed all my assignments. I spoke up in the classes and sometimes challenged the tutors and nothing terrible happened. You know, it's never too late to try something if you're able to.' After getting her degree, she took a year off and then returned to university to study for a master's degree.

Happiness might be difficult to find in tough times but this doesn't mean you've lost the capacity to experience it as you will probably discover when your life becomes stable again. However, Ellis (2001: 36) suggests that you could 'look for the fun and enjoyment – not merely the pain and problems – of doing difficult things that are in your best interest. Try to focus on the joyous challenge of doing them, and not only on the trouble and effort.' For example, you may have isolated yourself since the break-up of your relationship and remain reluctant to go out and meet people – 'I don't feel like it. I've got nothing to say' – even though you know that moping around the house isn't really helping you to get over the break-up. So you force yourself to go to a party you've been invited to despite your low mood. You make conversation and find that your mood lifts and you manage to laugh at a few jokes. You realize that you have got things to say and you will 'feel like it' eventually if you're prepared to push yourself into social activity when you don't feel like it.

Self-acceptance

This means accepting yourself, warts and all, and avoiding any global evaluations or ratings of yourself (positive or negative) as these cannot capture the complexity, changeability and uniqueness of the person you are (e.g. if you believe that you're a success because you've been promoted or a failure because you haven't been, do the words 'success' or 'failure' accurately and totally sum you up and your life past, present and future?). Self-acceptance means you refuse to rate yourself on the basis of your traits, actions, achievements or disappointments but you do rate those aspects of yourself which you wish to change or improve (e.g. 'I can accept myself for acting impulsively at times which brings more problems than I would like. However, I'm working hard to remind myself to think before I act, so I wait 48 hours to see if it still seems a good idea. It usually doesn't.'). If you condemn yourself for having a problem, you actually get two problems for the price of one: the original problem which you're trying to deal with (losing money on a get rich quick scheme which you could ill-afford to do) while dragging along the ball and chain of self-condemnation which is likely to distract from your problem-solving efforts ('I'm utterly pathetic for allowing myself to be so easily deceived. How could I have done this to myself?'). How many problems do you want?

Self-acceptance does not imply complacency – if you can accept yourself, then why bother to struggle for anything in life? You can be as ambitious as you want, work as hard as you want, and with self-acceptance guiding the way you're unlikely to worry excessively about taking risks (not foolish ones) which might result in failure or rejection. Also, you're unlikely to let success go to your head as your personal worth is not tied to achieving it (success and defeat are not to be taken too seriously). In fact, if you do act complacently about self-acceptance it is unlikely you actually understand the concept or have absorbed it into your outlook. To really understand and internalize it you need to put yourself in a range of situations where you are likely to be criticized, rejected and ridiculed – people are putting *you* down, not just your actions. This will enable you to determine the strength of your conviction in the concept of self-acceptance: is it lip service or committed service you're demonstrating?

For example, I have given presentations on CBT to therapists from other approaches who don't like it or are hostile to it – hostile audiences are more likely to be disparaging about CBT and its practitioners (e.g. 'CBT deals superficially with problems, giving psychological first aid so to speak, but there is no real depth and complexity to what you do because all you're teaching is positive thinking [this is not CBT]. That's all you do, isn't it? Teach positive thinking. It's not a proper training in psychotherapy like we undertake.'). I practise self-acceptance and acceptance of others (i.e. I accept them but not always their views or behaviour) in the face of these comments and usually engage in a vigorous discussion with my detractors. I've learnt to take these kinds of comments in my stride, which wasn't always the case earlier in my career.

Internalizing self-acceptance provides long-term psychological stability and quickens the process of self-righting when your life takes some unexpected knocks as you won't have to haul up your self-esteem from the low point to which it has fallen. As Hauck (1991: 32) states:

> There is only one technique you need to follow if you wish to avoid feelings of inferiority, low self-respect, low self-esteem, and low self-worth. To cure yourself of these conditions, do one thing: *never rate yourself or others*. Nothing else is needed. (original italics)

Having said all of the above, some clients believe that it's impossible never to rate oneself and pursuing this strategy with them proves unproductive, so an alternative viewpoint is to develop a multidimensional identity to face life's challenges, thereby avoiding putting all your eggs (i.e. your worth) in one basket (e.g. 'My work is everything to me') which would leave you much more vulnerable to self-condemnation when adversity strikes (you lose your job). Also, with a multidimensional identity an important loss in your life would probably be viewed in relative, not absolute, terms as the other aspects or dimensions of yourself would provide the sense of a continuing identity. A unidimensional or rigid identity is likely to view this important loss as absolute, leading to a loss of identity.

Teaching self-acceptance to my clients is my preference. I'm not keen on helping people to raise their self-esteem as what rises also falls when you make your self-worth conditional (esteem is derived from the Latin root *aestimare* 'to estimate') on certain requirements being present in your life (e.g. achieving your ideal weight, having lots of friends, a good job, a loving partner, well-behaved children, regular holidays). This gives the impression of the self as a stock market with your personal stock or value highly sensitive and acutely responsive to changing conditions in your life. If some of the desirable conditions that bolster your self-esteem disappear from your life, you're in danger of activating and being ensnared by your negative core beliefs (e.g. 'I'm repulsive when I'm overweight' or 'I've failed as a parent as my children are behaving terribly'). Self-acceptance is not based on favourable conditions being present in your life in order to validate your self-worth. If self-acceptance does have an identity, it is the acknowledgement of yourself as a fallible (imperfect), complex and unrateable human being and this view stays constant whatever the circumstances in your life (Neenan and Dryden, 2004).

Self-belief

Within reason, you're able to move your life in the direction you want it to go rather than see your life as being controlled by external forces which you have little influence over (e.g. respectively, 'If I want to get fit, then I know I'll be able to do it' versus 'Well, I'd like to be fit but, you know, things get in the way, the time just goes, and one thing leads to another and somehow I never can get round to it'). How do you build self-belief? By setting yourself a series of desired goals and showing yourself that you can achieve them or most of them. Make sure that some of these goals will be difficult to achieve otherwise your self-belief is unlikely to strengthen if you feel underwhelmed by easy goal achievement. Each time you achieve a goal you gain more confidence in your abilities – you do what you say you're going to do rather than make promises you don't deliver on.

Self-belief is inextricably linked with self-discipline, i.e. the ability to stay focused on your goals and carry out the actions required to get you there including overcoming blocks you encounter. Self-belief without self-discipline is having big dreams which are never realized. You are able to balance successfully your short- and long-term interests so neither one is neglected (e.g. if possible, I work on this book every day in order to meet the publisher's deadline without neglecting my other and more immediate responsibilities, so my mind is focused on both the present and the future). Also, self-belief encourages you to see that setbacks and failures are inevitable in life but provide you with valuable opportunities for learning and self-development instead of viewing them as 'What's wrong with me?' exercises in self-condemnation. However, self-belief can become:

- *self-rigidity* if you believe you must achieve all of your goals – failure is intolerable – thereby making your self-worth conditional on achieving them with all the problems this entails (see above section on self-acceptance).
- *self-deception* if you don't listen to the views of respected friends and colleagues who, for example, point out that you're

riding for a fall with the long hours you put in at work ('It won't happen to me'). I once saw a client who wanted to be a professional singer and she told me that all the professionals in the music business she had consulted informed her that she didn't have the vocal talent to succeed (her mother complained 'that she just won't listen to anyone and is making herself ill'). My client listed the singers who had been written off as talentless 'but then proved everyone wrong. That's what I'm going to do'. As far as I'm aware, she hasn't made any headway in achieving pop chart success (her goal).

- *self-absorption* where you're only interested in yourself. Having to spend time and effort listening to others' views rapidly bores and irritates you and your conversations are engineered to be strictly self-referential, i.e. you quickly bring the focus back to yourself. This is bound to alienate more people than it attracts.
- *self-inflation* when you praise yourself beyond your current accomplishments and proclaim that nothing is too hard for you to do. Others find it hard to take you seriously.
- *elimination of self-doubt.* You believe that entertaining doubt in your thinking will erode your self-belief to the point where you question all your judgements and this will lead to your eventual undoing ('I don't have faith in myself any more'). Attempting to eliminate self-doubt can create a totalitarian system of thinking whereby any internal or external dissent is stamped on ('I won't be cross-examined on my decisions!'). Self-doubt is part of self-belief as you're not afraid to examine what you're doing or the decisions you've made, and you sometimes conclude that you're wrong and fresh thinking and action is called for.

Humour

A sense of humour helps you to find light moments in dark times in order to bear the unbearable. Viktor Frankl, survivor of the Nazi concentration camps, called humour 'another one of the soul's weapons in the fight for self-preservation' (1985: 63). He said that humour enabled him and others to rise above the barbarous circumstances of the camps for very brief but precious periods. In his book *Hammer and Tickle* (2008), Ben Lewis looks at how people used jokes as acts of rebellion against the grimness of life under communist rule in Russia and eastern Europe. For example:

QUESTION: What is colder than the cold water in Romania?
ANSWER: The hot water.

Away from genocidal and tyrannical regimes and back to the resilience of everyday life, humour encourages you not to take yourself and your ideas too seriously, thereby helping you to step back and observe circumstances more objectively. Unlike practical jokes or sarcastic remarks which are used to make fun of or mock others, humour brings pleasure to both sides – those dispensing it and those receiving it (Vaillant, 1993) – and can help to defuse tense situations and bring a sense of solidarity to the challenges that you and others are facing.

Keeping things in perspective

This involves not jumping to gloomy or catastrophic conclusions every time a setback or difficulty is encountered. Instead, events are appraised in a calm and measured way that enables you to see what options you have to deal with them. When events are not kept in perspective, extreme thinking often emerges (e.g. 'It's all my fault' – no other factors contributed to the adverse outcome; 'It's awful' – nothing could ever be worse; 'I'll never get over it' – you believe you have predicted accurately how the rest of your life will unfold; 'I'll never understand how to do this' – you assume you won't be able to learn and apply new skills; or 'I'll always be alone' – you imagine no one will ever want you).

A lot of my time in therapy is spent acting as a cognitive guide, i.e. showing clients how to move away from their extreme thinking and towards the centre ground of balanced thinking where new and helpful perspectives can be discovered and discussed. For example, a client who says 'It's all my fault that my son's marriage failed' is making godlike assumptions of omnipotence (she has the power to control her son's life). By listing as many factors as possible that contributed to the demise of the marriage (e.g. her son being out of work, his heavy drinking, his financial debts, frequent rows with his wife, his wife's affair, parental interference from both sides of the marriage) she realized eventually that her ability to influence, let alone control, her son's life and all the circumstances affecting his marriage was severely limited. If she was indeed able to control her son's life, then happiness, not unhappiness, would be his reward. She accepted that she may have interfered too much in the marriage but this alone did not bring about its end.

Emotional control

This is the ability to moderate your intense feelings not only to stay focused in stressful situations but also to display consistent behaviour across a range of situations rather than people not knowing what mood you will be in from one moment to the next. It is important to point out that emotional control is not emotional suppression (i.e. trying to avoid revealing your feelings) but a proportionate response to a particular situation (e.g. asking someone politely but firmly to let you finish, without interruptions, the point you're making instead of shouting and hurling verbal abuse at him). Lack of emotional control usually wins few friends: 'Research shows that people who lack the ability to regulate their emotions have a hard time building and maintaining relationships. There are probably many reasons why this is so, the most basic of which is that negativity is a turnoff. People don't like to spend time with people who are angry, sullen, or anxious' (Reivich and Shatté, 2003: 37). The quickest way to start developing greater emotional control is to remember that you feel as you think – 'What am I telling myself to make me so upset about this issue?' This can be done in a structured way through the use of the ABC model which I described in Chapters 2 and 3:

A = adversity
B = beliefs
C = consequences – emotional and behavioural

Once you have identified the self-defeating belief(s), examine it in the way I also described in the same chapters: is your belief rigid or flexible, realistic or unrealistic, helpful or unhelpful, and would you teach your belief to others?

Support from others

You're able to ask for or accept support without seeing it as a sign of personal weakness. People who are compulsively self-reliant would usually view support in this way. Support from others, which can extend beyond your family and friends, provides fresh infusions of problem-solving ideas to replace the stale ones which you may have become stuck with, encourages you to persist in overcoming the roadblocks in your life, offers emotional release from pent-up feelings, provides the reassurance that you're not alone in the world and reaffirms your belief in yourself. In these ways, support from others acts as a buffer against the harsh impact of adversity. But don't forget to offer support to others in their time of need, otherwise you might come to be seen by them as leech-like, i.e. draining their emotional resources when you're struggling against the odds, but 'mysteriously' unavailable when they seek your help.

Support from others can be counterproductive: they burden you with their own misfortunes while you're struggling with your own; they become overly protective of you thereby undermining the development of your own resilience-building skills to deal with noxious events; they keep on being cheerfully optimistic thereby closing down the conversation every time you express your doubts and worries which may imply that the real message from them is 'Stop whining and get on with it!'; and they keep regaling you with their own tales of how 'I faced and overcame adversity' which is meant to impress and inspire you though you may become bored with having to be the reluctant audience for such tales (I fall into this trap when I lecture my son along the lines of 'When I was your age . . . hard work . . . self-discipline . . . times were hard . . . money in short supply', which usually produces in him eye-rolling and yawning.) Support from others is not an unqualified advantage. Assess the quality of the support being offered and whether it is likely to help or hinder you in dealing with your current difficulties.

Curiosity

You're eager to try things out, make discoveries, you like asking questions to increase your knowledge and understanding of the world around you. You maintain in adulthood a childlike curiosity about the world and its wonders. Siebert (2005: 95) states that 'an automatic openness to absorb new information epitomizes survivor resiliency. Curiosity is a valuable habit.' A question I ask my clients is: 'Are you curious about what you need to do to achieve your desired changes?' Replies range from 'of course' to 'no'; the latter reply stimulates my curiosity. To help bring about these desired changes, it's important to see that many of your thoughts and beliefs are hypotheses, not facts, about yourself and your life (e.g. you can't change your age (fact) but your belief that you could never live alone is a hypothesis waiting to be tested). You can test your beliefs by carrying out experiments (e.g. phoning your friend to determine the accuracy of your belief 'If I contact her after such a long period of silence she won't be interested in seeing me again'). It is important to remember that you can't know in advance the result of an experiment, so don't pin all your hopes on a particular outcome such as 'She's got to be as interested as I am in meeting again'. Foster open-mindedness with experiments so that whatever happens is of interest to you rather than seeing the outcome as either success or failure (e.g. your friend is not interested in meeting again but at least you made the effort to find out and can now close that particular file).

Those who lack curiosity and want to stay within the confines of the safe and predictable are likely to feel threatened by anything unfamiliar and display non-resilient responses when unexpected events strike ('Make it go away. I don't want to have to deal with it'). Additionally, displaying curiosity can sound like too much physical and/or mental effort ('Being curious is tiring. I get information overload very quickly. Why put yourself through that?'). Lack of fresh, challenging and exciting sensory input can dull and degrade the activity of your brain. Neuroscience has discovered the lifelong plasticity of the human brain:

> Environment [along with genetic factors] also has a major influence on neural [nerve] circuits. Experiences cause structural changes in the brain, sculpting synapses [gaps between nerve cells across which impulses pass] in profound ways. This 'plasticity' of the brain has been demonstrated by neuroscientists over the past decades . . . Our brains are not set in their structures by the genes we inherit but are continuously molded during the course of our lives . . . we are not prisoners of our DNA.
>
> (Groopman, 2006: 189–190)

This brain moulding or plasticity is based on acquiring new experiences and facing challenges to stimulate your brain (a brain-healthy lifestyle): 'These [brain] changes contribute to an increase in what is called your brain reserve. Research suggests that the more brain reserve, the more resistant the brain is to age-related or disease-related damages' (Michelon, 2008: 5). Armed with this knowledge of brain plasticity and how to maintain it, the usual advice is 'use it or lose it'. According to Csikszentmihalyi (1997), curiosity can be cultivated in some of the following ways:

1   *Try to be surprised by something every day.* For example, engaging in conversation at the bus stop or in the supermarket queue when your normal tendency is to remain quiet.

2   *Try to surprise at least one person every day.* For example, compliment someone on their appearance who would be 'shocked' and pleased to hear it from you or stay talking to your parents after Sunday dinner instead of your usual pattern of rushing home as soon as it's over.

3   *Write down each day what surprised you and how you surprised others.* Writing down your daily 'surprises' can help to keep them fixed in time rather than lost in the mists of time through relying on your memory. Also, you can reread them and enjoy again the experiences and what you learnt from them.

4   *When something strikes a spark of interest, follow it.* It was only when I did some background reading before writing this book that I became aware of the concept of brain plasticity. I was previously aware of keeping the brain active throughout life rather than 'boring it to death' through sameness or inaction and I'm reading more about the subject to broaden my understanding of it.

These four suggestions, if implemented, should help you to 'feel a stirring of possibilities under the accustomed surface of daily experiences. It is the gathering of creative energy, the rebirth of curiosity that has been atrophied since childhood' (Csikszentmihalyi, 1997: 348).

Problem-solving skills

This refers to the ability to identify and remove both internal and external blocks to change. Internal blocks might be anger, guilt or anxiety and external blocks might be financial debt, not meeting your performance targets or conflict with a work colleague. It is best to work on internal or emotional problem solving first before focusing on external or behavioural problem solving. It's hard to think of practical steps to take to sort out your problems when you're emotionally distressed. The emotional problem solving can be achieved through the use of the ABC model in order to identify, challenge and change the beliefs underlying your distressing feelings. I have explained the ABC model several times in this book, so in this section I want to focus on practical problem solving using the ADAPT model (Nezu et al., 2007).

Rosemary had a particular business client who got angry and shouted at her during contract negotiations which resulted in her making herself passive and placatory in his presence ('Maybe it's my fault he's like that and also I'm afraid to lose his business'). In the emotional problem-solving part of the therapy, she accepted that his anger was generated by him based on reasons that belonged to him, not put there by her. As part of standing up for herself, she was now prepared to lose his business rather than be spoken to in that way.

A = attitude: 'I'm now better prepared to deal with this issue. I feel optimistic about finding a solution.'

D = defining the problem and setting a realistic goal(s): 'The problem has been allowing him to shout at me because I didn't object to it. He does it every time we have a meeting, so it's likely to be difficult to get him to stop. My goal is for the meetings to be conducted in a professional manner, with give and take on both sides, but no shouting.'

A = generating alternative solutions: 'So in what ways can I attempt to achieve my goal? Well I could [making a list]:

1   Tell him that losing his temper is no longer acceptable and that timeouts in the meeting will be called when he starts making himself angry.
2   Try to find out why he loses his temper.
3   Explain to him why I've been so passive in the meetings and hope he will understand my new approach.
4   Phone or email him to let him know the conditions for the next meeting.'

P = predicting the consequences and developing a solution plan: 'What are the likely consequences for each alternative solution in terms of helping me to reach my goal, and will I be able to carry out the chosen solutions? First, let me evaluate the possible solutions:

1   This could be a good idea. Hopefully, he'll feel embar-
    rassed when I suggest the timeouts.
2   Yes. This might bring something to light that we need to
    discuss, but I'm definitely not his therapist!
3   No. I'm not going to seek his approval as I will put myself
    in a subordinate position again.
4   Yes. I will contact him to inform him of the new arrange-
    ments and let him know the worm has turned.

I'll try one, two and four and combine them into one solution.
And yes, I do believe that I will be able to carry it out. I really
want to get this problem sorted out.'

T = trying out the solution to see if it works: 'Well, I did phone
him and told him what would happen if he lost his temper. He
got a bit grumpy and said I didn't make my points clear at the
meetings, so I said I would do my best to rectify this if he told
me non-angrily which points they were. At the meeting when
he started to get grumpy – he was no longer really angry – I
suggested a short break so he could regain his self-control. He
didn't want a break and his grumpiness quickly disappeared. I
think he was embarrassed that I was staying in control and he
wasn't. Anyway, he never apologized for his angry outbursts
but I eventually got the contract. I wouldn't have been upset if
I'd lost it because I've made some welcome changes in myself.
You know, in the end I won three contracts: rewrote my own
contract to stop blaming myself for his behaviour, successfully
renegotiated the contract regarding his behaviour at the
meetings, and then won the business contract. Not bad at all.'

   If the initial solutions you try out are unsuccessful, experiment
with others on your list or think of some new ones including
seeking input from others. Additionally, if your emotional distress
intrudes again, go back to the ABC model to pinpoint the distress-
producing belief.

Absorbing interests

'Most people . . . tend to be happier when vitally absorbed in
something outside of themselves' (Walen et al., 1992: 6–7). These
interests provide an idyllic contrast with the mundane responsi-

bilities of daily living. Remember not to become obsessed or overly preoccupied with these activities as this is likely to throw your life off balance resulting in other important, but not so absorbing, activities being neglected (e.g. always on the golf course rather than carrying out the DIY tasks you promised to do). A passion for some hobby or interest powerfully and joyfully reminds you of the crucial difference between really living and merely existing, as a client once remarked to me when she discovered the wonders of classical music, particularly Mozart and Beethoven. You may have no idea what might interest you and therefore feel stymied. A way round this block is to try out different activities until something takes your fancy. You won't know what you're interested in until you allow yourself to find out!

Finding meaning

'This dynamic of meaning making is, most researchers agree, the way resilient people build bridges from present-day hardships to a fuller, better constructed future. Those bridges make the present manageable, for lack of a better word, removing the sense that the present is overwhelming' (Coutu, 2003: 10). Building these bridges to the future takes time as meaning usually slowly emerges from your struggles with adversity rather than them being rapidly built – meaning making is swiftly achieved. A client I saw thought she would be forever inconsolable over the death of her son (he was killed by a drunk driver), but one day while walking her dogs in the neighbouring fields, 'It hit me with tremendous force that my son would not want me to carry on like this and would urge me to get on with my life. I had told myself this on many occasions and so had others but in some strange, indefinable way I suddenly realized the truth of it on that day. It was a turning point. When I got back home I set about rejoining the human race by asking a friend over for coffee and things moved on from there.'

Some clients believe that nothing good can ever come from anything bad and turn their faces against the search for meaning in the resilience sense yet, unfortunately, sink into the helplessness of being a victim – a meaning which can keep them trapped in their endless complaining about the unfairness of life. Others may impose a synthetic (i.e. not genuinely believed) meaning on to events in the hope that this will make them feel better. 'Bad things happen to everyone sooner or later no matter how well you've led your life', but at a deeper level they still insist, 'But it shouldn't have happened to me!'

Adaptability

This is the ability to determine how best to adjust your thinking and behaviour to current challenging circumstances in order to find a constructive way of dealing with them (e.g. tailoring expenditure to a much reduced income since you lost your job in order to avoid slipping into debt, or seeing your children leave home as an opportunity to expand your horizons rather than mope around complaining of an empty life). Being adaptable can mean the difference between life and death as it was for prisoners of war in Japanese prison camps in the Second World War:

> Most men agreed that the key to survival was adaptability. It was essential to recognise that this new life, however unspeakable, represented a reality which must be acknowledged. Those who pined for home, who gazed tearfully at photos of loved ones, were doomed. [According to one POW] There was a weeding-out thing. The ones who cried went early. [Another POW commented] I made a conscious decision that this was the new life, and I had to get on with it. I just dismissed the old one, as if it didn't exist. The tragedy was that so many people couldn't accommodate themselves.
>
> (Hastings, 2007: 379)

Whatever the new and usually unwelcome reality in your life, determine what needs to be done to steer yourself successfully through this unfamiliar landscape. For example, what personal changes have to be made? What knowledge and/or skills need to be acquired? Who are the people to ask for their advice as they've been through what you're now experiencing? Keep focused on your goals and monitor your progress towards achieving them rather than allowing yourself to be sidetracked continually by giving in to the anger, for example, you feel welling up inside you every time you ponder on the unfairness of what's happened to you. You can acknowledge your negative emotions but choose not to engage with them every time they surface; in this way, you continue in your goal-directed striving. See setbacks to your progress as learning opportunities to inform your next move, not as defeats that are likely to make you give up (a description of progress would include dealing with setbacks). Persaud (2001: 115) notes that 'the more adaptable you are to a wide range of environments, situations, people and predicaments, the more mentally healthy you are . . . Given that the world is being transformed at a faster and faster pace, the need for adaptable people has never been more imperative'.

But remember, your capacity to adapt to change is not unlimited. There will usually come a 'stop-the-world-I-want-to-get-off' time when you feel exhausted or overwhelmed by the pace and/or amount of change you've had or are continuing to deal with (Hoopes and Kelly, 2004). Your psychological and physical resources for managing change have been depleted and you need a period of rest and reflection to rebuild your adaptive capacity or, if this is not possible, perhaps seek professional guidance to show you better ways of coping with change. You can learn to increase your adaptive capacity, eke it out so to speak, by, among other things, accepting that change is necessary or unavoidable in this situation, drawing up a plan of action that will help to produce a productive 'fit' between yourself and your new circumstances (such as having to retrain after losing your job), and not insisting that the change process should be easy or painless.

The quickest way to deplete your personal resources for coping with inescapable change is to refuse to accept the new conditions in your life and focus all your energies on resisting them. A form of 'won't power', a self-defeating and maybe self-deceiving form of willpower, that seeks to maintain the status quo in your life even when you see it is slowly or rapidly vanishing before your eyes (e.g. refusing to accept your marriage is coming to an end by continuing to act as if you're still getting on with each other. Your 'Have you ironed a shirt for me and what's for dinner?' questions are answered by your wife's scornful 'Are you being serious?' look which reinforces her determination to move out as soon as possible).

You might argue that being adaptable means avoiding those things that you fear: 'I adapt myself to the environment by always using the stairs instead of the lift in case I get stuck in it. The bonus is climbing all those stairs keeps me fit. More people could use the stairs as part of their fitness routine.' The flaw in this argument is that the person is depriving herself of the choice to use the lift such as when she's carrying her shopping; instead of changing her behaviour in order to give herself a more flexible response to the situation, she 'shrinks' the environment to fit her problem (Persaud, 2001).

The shifting balance of strengths

The list of strengths discussed above is interdependent and therefore it is difficult to determine which are primary in order for the other ones to develop. For example, are problem-solving skills acquired because you first have the high frustration tolerance (HFT) to learn them, or does HFT develop once you have the self-belief that you're largely in control of your life and can take it in the direction that you want? I would liken this discussion to the question of the chicken and egg – which one came first? Instead of scratching your head over this question, determine what resilience strengths you do have, which ones might need bolstering (e.g. not being curious enough restricts the range of problem-solving options that could be open to you), and what strengths you might need to develop (e.g. you're still reluctant to seek help when you become bogged down in your difficulties because you believe it shows weakness).

Even if you appear to have an impressive array of strengths, Flach (2004) remarks that there is unlikely to be a perfect balance amongst them: some will be practised more than others. For example, you may have vitally absorbing interests but rather poor emotional control when interrupted while immersed in them. You may be very curious about trying new experiences but usually avoid those where you might be criticized or rejected, thereby not making much effort to internalize self-acceptance. These underused ones need your attention too. Even the strengths you pride yourself on can desert you at times, such as your self-belief becoming rather shaky when events are tougher to deal with than you anticipated. Flach (2004) suggests that you periodically assess your strengths and limitations and decide what adjustments may be needed. You can't expect your level of resilience to remain consistently high whatever challenges you're facing.

Keep on keeping on

In this section I would like to focus on resilience in action through the example of my colleague, Professor Windy Dryden of London University. His story illustrates most of the strengths I have discussed.

I demonstrated a resilient attitude when in 1983 I took voluntary redundancy from the University of Aston in Birmingham.
I thought that it wouldn't be too difficult to find another job in
academia. How wrong I was! In fact, it took me over two years
and 54 job rejections before I found my next post at the
University of London. People who hear this story think I must
have been depressed, but I wasn't. They usually say that they
probably would have been depressed if what happened to me
had happened to them instead. Their usual focus is on how
their self-esteem or self-confidence would have taken such a
battering from all the job rejections and, therefore, would have
concluded that there must have been something seriously
wrong with them – they were bad, incompetent or useless
individuals; in other words, these job rejections would inevitably lead to self-rejection, there could be no other outcome. I
became neither depressed nor gave up looking for a job.

However, I was disappointed and frustrated at times with
how long it was taking to get another job, my own earlier
expectations now laughably naive. I'm certainly not trying to
claim I'm a superior person because I persisted in the face of so
much rejection but, looking back and it's only in retrospect
that it becomes really clear, what I was demonstrating
throughout this period was a set of resilient-like responses. To
start with, I had a healthy attitude based on:

- *Self-acceptance*: 'Job rejections do not devalue my worth
  as a person. My worth as a person stays constant whatever
  happens in my life.' Self-acceptance kept me psychologically stable during this period as I kept reminding myself
  that an event or a series of events can never define me as a
  person. I'm unrateable.
- *Hope*: 'If I keep going I will find a worthwhile job in the
  end.' If hope goes, depression and inertia are likely to
  follow.

That was the C (thinking) part of CBT. I also engaged in
constructive behaviour (the B part) in order to support and
strengthen my beliefs. This behaviour was based on:

- *Perseverance*: I kept on applying for jobs, filling out appli-
  cation forms and attending interviews. The great truth

about perseverance is articulated by the philosopher Anthony Grayling (2002: 39): 'It is not what we get but what we become by our endeavours that makes them worthwhile.' While I was obviously happy to eventually get a job, it was knowing that I could endure that stiffened my spirit; no matter how many times I got knocked down, I got up again. I was determined to stay with it.

- *Involvement in personally meaningful activities.* At the same time as I was going through the job-finding process, I carried on writing and editing books, activities that are personally meaningful to me. Also, I reminded myself that disappointment in one area of my life doesn't have to spill over into other areas which, if it did, might impair the enjoyment of my writing projects.
- *Changing my behaviour in interviews.* I found it difficult at the time to get feedback on my interview performance, but I eventually discovered through back channels, you might say, that what I considered to be self-confidence was being seen by interview panels as arrogance. This piece of news came as a shock. It seemed I appeared aloof in the interviews, delivering my opinions from on high and I lacked warmth in my interactions with the interview panel. If this was the reason why I wasn't getting a job, I made up my mind to train myself in demonstrating humility in the interview process. This meant, for example, being attentive to what each panel member asked me and being more expansive in my replies to their questions rather than the somewhat curt pronouncements I may have previously made. I got a job soon after.
- *Using social support.* I was grateful for the support I received during my job wilderness years. My family and friends, particularly my wife, gave me the encouragement that allowed me to proceed in my own way instead of being constantly lectured by them on what I must be doing wrong or being compared unfavourably with colleagues who had left their jobs and had secured new ones fairly quickly. Their invaluable support demonstrated their faith in me, namely, that I would achieve my goal in the end.

So, what did I learn from my unexpectedly extended job-hunting period? First, it is important to persevere in the face of adversity, in both behaviour and attitude. Second, one's self is so much larger than the experiences that we face and thus to define one's worth at any point in time is detrimental to developing resilience. Third, it is important to involve oneself in life beyond the adversity even if one's mind is preoccupied with it – if you do this, your mind will eventually follow your behaviour. Fourth, get feedback from others whenever you can, otherwise you may be repeating errors that could be corrected. And finally, let others in to your struggles so they can support you and disengage from those who are unsupportive. I often look back with satisfaction to those two years, 1983 to 1985, and reflect on the strengths I displayed during that period which have kept me in good stead ever since.

Lasting strengths

Whether you have some of the strengths listed above or ones that I haven't included or a mixture of both, it's important not to let them decay through neglect or infrequent use. Set yourself fresh challenges on a regular basis as these will take you out of your comfort zone where psychological stagnation is likely to occur if you linger too long within it. Moving into and through your discomfort zone will encourage you to reach deeper into yourself to uncover those strengths that Windy Dryden spoke about. The more you practise such behaviour, the more habitual will be your resilient response to life events, whether they're small irritations or major crises. Additionally, brain plasticity (the lifelong ability of the brain to reorganize neural pathways) is maintained through learning, and this learning is derived from new experiences. Don't make your life 'brain deadening' by being risk averse, i.e. never willingly stepping outside of the familiar and routine. An arena where routine may be frequently shaken up by the relentless pace of change is the workplace, which I focus on in the next chapter.

Chapter 6

Resilience in the workplace

Introduction

It seems that every day there are stories in the media about the ever-increasing prevalence of stress in the workplace, its cost to employers and the economy as a whole, as well as the harmful physical and psychological effects on those individuals experiencing it. Stress is one of the major reasons employees cite for their absence from work, and stress-related absence is increasing (Chartered Institute of Personnel and Development, 2008). Employees complain of, among other things, longer hours which adversely affect home life, job insecurity, tedious and tiring commuting, increased demands but with fewer staff to meet them, too many meetings, email overload, difficult colleagues, uncaring and incompetent managers, meaningless targets, and rapid technological changes they have to keep up with as well as the faster pace of work these technologies require. So what is stress? It can be defined as occurring when pressures that you face exceed your ability to cope with them (Palmer and Cooper, 2007). A CBT-based view of stress would focus on how you appraise both the challenges you're facing and your ability to cope with them in order to understand more fully your current difficulties.

For example, taking on some of the duties of a colleague who is on holiday can lead you to believe that you're overloaded with work (too much pressure) and, instead of prioritizing what needs to be done, you jump from task to task without completing any of them as you think they're all equally important to work on (your rushing around like a headless chicken coping style means you're exhausted at the end of each working day and this exhaustion is carried over into the weekends, thereby making you feel demoralized about facing the new working week). This cognitive focus on the contribution you make to your stress levels is not meant to let employers and government off the hook – they too have their part to play in managing stress in the workplace – but to show you that by thinking and acting differently about the challenges you face, you can learn to be more resilient, much less stressed, at work.

Another definition of stress is offered by Dato (2004: 12) which he calls the Law of Stress: 'This law states that *stress is the difference between pressure of any kind and adaptability*, or *Stress = Pressure –* [minus] *Adaptability*. This law clearly implies that *stress = unadaptability*' (original italics). I remember a client who refused point-blank to adapt to the departmental changes made by a new management team. She went off sick with stress but, more specifically and accurately, was depressed and angry about her traditional ways of working being 'swept aside. I love my job, but I definitely don't like these new management ideas'. Despite being offered a generous financial package (the new team were eager to keep her), she refused to return to work until the old ways of working were reinstated. Clearly, this was a pipe dream. She never returned to that company and our sessions fizzled out to the accompaniment of her ceaseless lament, 'Why does everything always keep on changing?' My usual reply was that 'Nothing is constant', and this can be a hard but necessary truth to accept if one wants to remain employable. Adaptability to challenging and changing circumstances is one of the key strengths underpinning resilience that I discussed in Chapter 5. It is important to point out that adaptability has its ethical limits. I'm not recommending that you allow yourself to be exploited by your employer or tolerate a bullying boss all in the name of adaptability. This would be 'adaptability' to one's own detriment.

In this chapter and the next two, my clients' stories follow a similar pattern. Their difficulties are outlined particularly focusing on where they're stuck in their thinking and behaviour. Therapy helps them to widen their perspective so they can see other more constructive ways of dealing with their problems. The constructive ways are adopting flexible attitudes and behaviours to guide these individuals through their struggles so that they emerge from them psychologically stronger and wiser. The learning to be extracted from their struggles is encapsulated in each section heading.

There's always more than one way of looking at a problem

A senior police officer I saw, Raymond, was very angry that his new boss was making his working life difficult and thereby interfering greatly with what he thought was going to be a pleasant winding down process to retirement in a few years' time. He said he had dealt with many difficult and sometimes very unpleasant situations in his career, but this present one didn't appear to have a solution (retiring earlier was out of the question as he wanted to collect his full pension). However, he was determined to find one:

RAYMOND: I don't want to fall at the last hurdle, so to speak, but why does he behave like that, finding fault with almost everything I do? I wouldn't behave like that. What's wrong with him? My wife gets fed up with me moaning about him. I feel stressed out having to deal with him every day.

MICHAEL: Well, we could speculate about his motives for behaving that way or explore some ideas on how to manage yourself better in your relationship with him. Which one might be more productive at this stage?

RAYMOND: I'm tempted to say let's focus on him.

MICHAEL: Whose behaviour is within your control to change – yours or his?

RAYMOND: Well, obviously mine. Why does my behaviour need to change? I'm not the problem, he is!

MICHAEL: You are the problem to some extent. Shall I explain? [Client nods.] People who are angry about others' behaviour are usually demanding that these others shouldn't be the way they undoubtedly are. It's like constructing an internal brick wall [tapping my forehead] which you keep on banging your head against every day – 'He shouldn't behave like that!' – but without any corresponding change in your boss's behaviour to show that your strategy is working. So you've got two problems for the price of one: his continuing difficult-to-deal-with behaviour and your anger about it.

RAYMOND: I probably have got my own brick wall but it sounds like you're supporting his behaviour.

MICHAEL: I'm not doing that – just pointing out, however unpalatable it might be to you, that *his* behaviour flows from *his* values and viewpoint, not yours. If he shared your values, then this problem presumably wouldn't have arisen.

RAYMOND: So if I accept that point . . .

MICHAEL: Without having to like it.

RAYMOND: . . . and without having to like it, that he is the way that he is, is my anger supposed to suddenly vanish?

MICHAEL: Not suddenly vanish, but you can achieve a significant reduction in the frequency, intensity and duration of your anger if you accept it's your responsibility to change it, not for him to change his behaviour first. That's where you're stuck. Can you imagine in what ways your life at work would be different if you dismantled this internal brick wall?

RAYMOND: Not really. I can't see past the anger at the present time, but I want to.

MICHAEL: Maybe I'm jumping ahead here. As an experiment, see if you can stand back from your anger, notice it but don't engage with it, and observe – make notes if you wish – any changes in yourself and in your relationship with him.

RAYMOND: What if nothing happens and I can't stand back from it?

MICHAEL: Let's see what happens, whatever the outcome. When you do an experiment, you don't know in advance what the outcome will be.

RAYMOND: Okay, I've got nothing to lose but my anger. I'm sure if I tell my wife about my brick wall, she'll agree with you.

MICHAEL: Your wife might have some good ideas you're not listening to. Something else to consider is this: if you think your anger is justified because of his behaviour, he probably thinks his anger towards you is justified because of your behaviour.

RAYMOND: I hadn't considered that. I'm sure he does as he finds fault with my work quite frequently. You know, I came to the session today thinking the focus would be on him yet it's all about me. Interesting, but unsettling.

A rule of thumb in attempting to influence (not control) someone else's behaviour is to manage yourself first:

> The last thing you need after someone has done you an injustice is to do a greater injustice to yourself. Getting angrily upset over a frustration does not usually remove the frustration and always adds to your discomfort. In fact, most of the time the greatest distress comes not from what others do to us but from what we let our upsets do.
>
> (Hauck, 1980: 122)

Once Raymond accepted the idea that he made himself angry about his boss's behaviour, then the way became clear for marked changes in his own behaviour. He now saw work as a laboratory, rather than as purgatory, where he could try out new beliefs and behaviours. One new response he experimented with, as advocated by Ellis (1977), was to be nice when his boss displayed what Raymond perceived as obnoxious behaviour:

RAYMOND: I thought you were crazy when you suggested it. He doesn't know how to handle it. He's baffled by my behaviour but he's becoming much less obnoxious now. It's as if he's wilting in the face of my niceness and calmness though I still have days when the old angry impulses come flooding back but, thankfully, not for long. You know, I thought that fighting back would be asking him outside for a bout of fisticuffs [laughs].

MICHAEL: You are fighting back in a low-key, non-violent but determined way. The key question to ask: is it working?

RAYMOND: It is, but I had to clear away the red mist before I could see the range of options that might be helpful to me to deal with this problem. That range was wider than I ever thought. I still don't like him, and I even feel sorry for him at times because he's such a lousy manager, but now I feel that these last few years before I retire are controlled by me, not him, even though he's my boss. That is a most welcome change.

Stepping back from micromanagement and focusing on self-management

Francine was a new manager and wanted to make a good impression on her boss through demonstrating the efficiency of her team. Unfortunately, her view of team management meant micromanaging (i.e. controlling every aspect of a task or activity) the tasks she delegated to them. Francine's team felt resentful towards her micromanaging approach, believing that they 'couldn't be trusted' to complete the tasks without constant scrutiny and also for stifling any initiative they might want to show. She wanted to stop her micromanaging approach as she began to realize how demoralizing it was for them. However, she was worried about stepping back to let them get on with the delegated tasks but couldn't put her finger on the core of her worry, so we used the downward arrow technique (Burns, 1999) to find out. This technique follows the logical implications of each revealed thought by asking variations on 'Let's assume that's true . . . then what?' questions. These questions help clients to dig deeper into their thinking in order to pinpoint the underlying beliefs related to their concerns. To start her off, I asked Francine what was worrying in her mind (this is to orient her to look inwards for the source of her worry rather than outwards) if she stepped back from micromanaging her team:

'They might get things wrong.'
  ↓   'And if they do get things wrong, then what?'
'Then I'll have to sort it out.'
  ↓   'And if you have to sort it out?'
'That will increase my own workload.
I'll fall behind with my own important work.'
  ↓   'If you do fall behind with your own work,
           then what?'
'Then my boss will see I can't cope,
I can't run my department.'
  ↓   'And if he does think that, what does that
           mean to you?'
'It means that I'm incompetent, can't manage
properly, I shouldn't have been promoted.'

The irony was that through her micromanagement style she was already falling behind with completing her own work and staying late at the office to try and catch up. Whether she stepped back or kept a tight rein on her team, she feared being exposed as incompetent through the consequences of following each alternative. She felt trapped. This feeling of being trapped was actually a thought, not a genuine feeling (see distinctions between thoughts and feelings in Chapter 2, pp. 30–31), and therefore could be treated as a hypothesis (to be tested) instead of being viewed by her as a fact (unchangeable).

However, as I discussed in Chapter 5 in the section on problem-solving skills (pp. 85–87), emotional difficulties can block you from implementing action plans. In Francine's case, her worry that she would be exposed as incompetent as she was linking her performance to her self-worth ('I am my performance'). The first step was to decouple the self – too complex to be given a single global rating – from her performance which could be rated in order to improve it: 'I'm unrateable, but my current performance regarding my micromanagement style and falling behind with my own work can be rated as poor.' She could see the sense in this distinction as her fear of being viewed as incompetent was increasing her stress levels and thereby inhibiting clear, non-disturbed thinking about how to resolve this issue. With the focus switched from self to performance, she decided to step back from micromanagement and learn to tolerate the uncertainty of doing so by treating it as an experiment. She took the following actions:

- She announced to the team – much to their relief – a change in her management strategy. She wouldn't be able to assess properly their skills and strengths if she was continually peering over their shoulders but would hold regular reviews to monitor their progress with the delegated tasks.
- She reminded herself that she is still accountable for how the team performed with their delegated tasks – there is no delegate and forget.
- She did her best to refrain from taking over a task when a team member ran into trouble with it. In Chapter 1, under the section 'Resilience and behaviour' (pp. 11–12), I discussed the difference between action tendencies, i.e. how you may or may not act in a specific situation, and clear or completed actions, i.e. what you actually did in that situation. The powerful 'pull' of her action tendencies meant Francine wanted to say, 'I'll do it for you', but she held herself in check and, instead, asked the person questions to stimulate his problem-solving abilities because she kept in mind that her longer term goal was to improve the performance of the team, both individually and collectively: 'I found that part really hard as I wanted to snatch the tasks from them when they ran into trouble as I had these horrible images of them making ghastly mistakes which would put me in a bad light. But I'm glad I persisted in putting it back to them.' She kept reminding herself that coaching, not micromanaging, was the way forward as a team manager.
- Through delegation, she could make a more accurate assessment regarding which team member(s) could take over her duties when she was on holiday or ill as well as of their promotion potential.

By carrying out these actions, she was able to get on with her own important tasks, complete most of them within her deadlines, leave the office at a reasonable time and was now managing an empowered rather than a disgruntled team. Looking back, she said that it was clear that being trapped was only a state of mind. Looking at a problematic situation from an unfamiliar perspective – focusing on her performance not herself and taking risks to find new ways of working – now gave real meaning to what she had previously dismissed as a cliché when uttered by some of her colleagues, namely, that every obstacle you encounter can be transformed into an opportunity for learning and self-development. 'I'm going to do my best not to forget that lesson the next time I'm stumped over what to do with a particular issue,' she concluded.

The perils of trying to be perfect

Louise was a deputy head teacher in a primary school and worked so hard to please everyone that she was exhausted at the weekends and ill during the school holidays: 'I seem to save up all my illnesses and then collapse in the holidays.' She said that she put everything into doing her job. What was driving her so hard? She described herself as a perfectionist: always striving to achieve very high standards in order to avoid being criticized, disliked or rejected for poor performance. 'I start worrying about failing on the next task before I've completed the present one.' If she didn't put a foot wrong, then she would be liked, but she worried constantly that she may have said or done something wrong to upset someone. She spent a lot of her worrying time 'living' in the minds of her colleagues, wondering if she was fulfilling what she perceived as their expectations of her. In order to keep these expectations favourable, she would take on tasks that really belonged to the other teachers, including the head, which then ate considerably into her own time and often meant doing without coffee breaks and/or having much shortened lunch breaks and falling behind with her own work.

I asked her what beliefs lay at the core of her anxious striving: 'That I'm not good enough. I've thought that for a long time.' The 'evidence' she gave for this belief was that: her parents had high expectations of her which she believed she hadn't lived up to but couldn't recall them being overly critical towards her; she didn't excel at school; she got a 'poor degree' instead of the first she wanted; and attributed her position as deputy head to 'luck', not competence. For these and other reasons, she saw herself as a 'fraud'. However, if she could achieve her exceptionally high standards, then this would give her respite from self-criticism until the whole cycle started again the next day. When she fell below these standards this confirmed in her mind that she was indeed a fraud, but somehow was 'getting away with it' (her colleagues hadn't yet noticed she was deceiving them). No wonder she was depressed, demoralized and exhausted. Knaus (2002: 52) suggests that the perfectionist's philosophy is: 'I must be what I think I should be, or I'm nothing at all.' This is a rigid ('must be', no other options are to be considered) and extreme ('I'm nothing', a throwaway self) view of oneself.

You might think that with all these problems, particularly their long history, Louise would need long-term therapy to sort them out rather than me encouraging her to develop a resilient outlook as a means of problem solving. As Maddi and Khoshaba (2005: 43) point out:

> As long as you can use life experiences to grow, psychologically and socially, you can learn to be resilient as an adult. Resist falling into the trap of thinking that once you reach adulthood, you are what you are, and nothing will change that. Hardiness [their term for resilience] research . . . indicates that adolescents and adults can learn to be resilient.

Louise wanted to design a change programme as soon as possible once she perceived that I understood her problems. We identified the strengths she could use to help her change, namely, her diligence, persistence in the face of difficulties, love of learning, and 'I don't want to waste my time and money in coming to see you if all I'm going to do is moan and complain about everything.' This last comment was good news. As Albert Einstein observed (quoted in Auerbach, 2006: 113): 'No problem can be solved from the same consciousness that created it.' In other words, most of therapy needs to be focused on developing new, problem-solving thinking instead of dwelling on old problem-perpetuating thinking.

The key change strategy was to develop new performance standards that were not linked to self-worth: evaluate the performance, not oneself on the basis of the performance. Her new standards were high but not too high (she was adamant that she didn't want to adopt what she considered were low or mediocre standards) and she would now aspire to achieve them. This would start the process of freeing herself from the mental straitjacket of having to achieve them. Compassion for herself was sadly lacking but she began to warm to the idea of accepting herself as a fallible (imperfect) human being who could be understanding and forgiving instead of condemning when she fell below her standards or was disliked by others. She also started practising being flexible in terms of how much time and effort a particular task required in relation to its importance: 'I used to think they were all equally important and therefore all had to be done equally well.' Her new, evolving outlook was summarized as 'Aim high, but be flexible and compassionate as well.'

She was a quick learner and willing to engage in experiments to test her new outlook. She carried out every experiment nervously, expecting the worst each time (experiencing considerable discomfort does not have to prevent you from moving towards your goals). For example, instead of obsessively going through reports she'd written to remove mistakes of any kind in order to forestall later criticism if one was discovered, she sent them out after a reasonable check within an agreed period. No criticisms were made; if there had been she would remind herself to focus on the error, not herself. On another occasion, while chairing a meeting, she politely interrupted a verbose colleague to remind her to keep to the agenda and 'the world didn't come to end'; her colleague merely nodded and complied with her request. Probably the most nerve-wracking of the experiments was saying 'no' when her colleagues and/or the head tried to push work on to her that belonged to them and stopping herself from taking it off them in the first place. Either way, she could end up being disliked or rejected, though she couldn't think of one person in her life, past or present, who had disliked or rejected her. She wasn't the kind of person who would provoke in others strong negative feelings towards her.

When she started pushing back the tasks to others, there was no revolt from her colleagues apart from one or two prickly comments from a particular teacher. Clawing back time for herself meant having regular coffee and dinner breaks and taking home much less work which then gave her more opportunity for engaging in pleasurable pursuits. When we discussed the results of the experiments, she was continually amazed 'that nothing much happens. No one comments on my new behaviour or is hostile to me. It's rather an anticlimax, something of a mystery.' An answer to this 'mystery', I suggested, might be that the other teachers had their own concerns to think about rather than being preoccupied with changes in Louise's behaviour; she may have lived too much in their minds but this didn't mean that they wanted to inhabit hers. Or they preferred to avoid interpersonal conflict. Whatever the reason, the important point was that the 'push back' strategy was working.

We had eight sessions over a three-month period. At the end of therapy, she felt she had developed 'more of a resilient spirit' but was still prone to worrying too much at times about not achieving her standards or being disliked by others. If she wanted to maintain and strengthen her gains from therapy, then she would need to act as her own lifelong therapist or coach. Like many of my clients and some I've already mentioned in this book, she wondered why she hadn't instituted these changes earlier in her life. The reason is simple but profound: because she didn't have the mindset or know-how then, unlike now, to achieve these changes.

Embrace discomfort as part of the change process

In this age of flexible working, one or two days a week working from home seems advantageous: no tedious commuting which can make you feel drained before you start work plus the commuting time saved; you can create your own comfortable space where you can really concentrate and think creatively, a blissful separation from the distractions, noise and interruptions of office life. That's the theory, but what can happen in practice is that you start procrastinating so that the tasks you planned to do don't get started or, if started, not completed.

Procrastination can be described as putting off until later (often an indefinite later) what our better judgement tells us ought to be done now and thereby incurring unwanted consequences through such dilatory behaviour. The 'putting off' occurs because you're seeking more interesting or pleasurable activities to engage in rather than experiencing now the discomfort, worry or difficulty associated with doing the avoided tasks. It is important to distinguish between procrastination and planned delay where, in the latter case, there are legitimate reasons for postponing action such as collecting more information about making an important decision (though this can segue into procrastination if you're worried about making the wrong decision). Also, it would be incorrect to dismiss procrastination as mere laziness because the latter behaviour is based on an unwillingness to exert yourself while the former behaviour frequently involves you doing other things, keeping busy, in order to avoid getting on with the priority tasks that require action now. In helping clients with their procrastination, it's important that I make an early start in identifying the current factors that maintain their dilatory behaviour and devising action plans to address these factors. Spending too much time talking about the causes and consequences of their procrastination is likely to prolong it in therapy.

Rob had his own publishing company. He had a youthful team whom he liked to 'spark off' to keep his energy levels high and stimulate new ideas. He said it 'was fun to go to work, there's a real buzz about the place'. Rob decided he would like to work from home one afternoon a week to give some 'quality attention' to an important project he was working on. Unfortunately, alone at home he felt the 'solitude oppressing me, draining my energy. I was paralysed. I didn't get any work done'. What work he did do was to make frequent cups of coffee, pace round the house, smoke more than he wanted to, look out of the window a lot, browse the internet, stare at his mobile phone hoping it would ring or he'd get a text message, and frequently check his emails. He was surprised and alarmed at how low his mood sank during the afternoon, only rising when his wife came home. He tried several more times in the following weeks to start the project at home, but each time his attempt ended in failure.

What was going wrong? Rob was keen to find out and correct it. He was an extrovert, so he obviously liked being with people, frequently the centre of attention, and enjoyed the warmth and laughter that came from these interactions; he wanted fun and excitement, being on the move, something always happening around him. Spending time alone, shut off from his usual sources of stimulation, he found he had no inner directed motivation to get on with his work and felt overwhelmed with the discomfort in trying to do so – hence his procrastination. To make matters worse from Rob's viewpoint, he now realized that even at work he would not stay for long in his office, often prowling around the building to see what was going on, or if he forced himself to concentrate for a long period he was hoping, sometimes desperately, to be interrupted so he could start 'buzzing' again. Consequently, his attention was frequently wandering away from the task at hand.

I pointed out to Rob that the more attributes he had made him more adaptable across a wider range of situations. Different aspects of himself can be emphasized in different situations depending on what's required of him – increasing his list of attributes depends on how willing he is to develop new ones. For example, I'm outgoing when I'm running training courses but seek solitude to write this book. I couldn't write it if I craved company all the time and I would a poor trainer if I kept squirming while in the spotlight. Being sociable and seeking solitude, depending on the circumstances, are what Siebert (2005: 130) calls counterbalanced qualities: 'The more [counterbalanced] pairs of traits you have [e.g. quiet and talkative, adventurous and cautious, friendly and aloof, rebellious and compliant], the more you have the mental and emotional flexibility essential for resiliency.' You don't have to be only one way, I concluded.

Rob listened in fascination to my brief lecture, could see the sense in what I was saying and said he was 'up for it' in wanting to be self-absorbed (introverted) when required. To put the icing on the cake for Rob, research shows that introverts are more task oriented than extroverts (Persaud, 2005), so if he developed his 'introvert side' there was a very good chance that he would be able to start and finish his important project in the quiet of his own home.

As a first step in this process of change, he agreed to give himself a daily dose of discomfort by spending time alone at home (his wife made herself scarce during these periods) and letting himself experience the physical and psychological agitation that followed being deprived of others' company. He could read, paint, listen to music or just sit there and think. He monitored his discomfort level to see how quickly or slowly it dropped from high to low. As he became used to his own company and learned to tolerate the discomfort of solitude, his discomfort level not only dropped more quickly but also didn't rise as high as on previous occasions: 'I was surprised. The anticipation was worse than the actual doing of it.' Remembering our discussions, he reminded himself that he was immersing himself in productive discomfort designed to help him achieve his goal as opposed to the unproductive discomfort involved in procrastination, i.e. feeling bad for not starting his project and wasting time. After a couple of weeks 'limbering up', he started on his project still feeling moderately uncomfortable but persisted nevertheless. Taking one afternoon off each week for a month, he finished the project. He was extremely pleased with achieving his goal.

What had he learnt? He said that what appeared intolerable eventually became tolerable and then enjoyable. He was beginning to appreciate the benefits of his own company ('I can relax and laugh with myself. Solitude can be liberating; it doesn't have to be oppressive.'). He liked the flexibility of moving between his extrovert and introvert sides when circumstances dictated. At work, he still prowled round the building chatting to his staff but when he secluded himself in his office to work, he really meant it now and stayed put, instructing his staff not to interrupt him unless it was urgent. If you want to develop resilience, then don't dodge experiencing discomfort:

> People with high frustration tolerance are going to experience less stress, accomplish more, and feel better about themselves. Facing up to your frustrations, building tolerance for them, and acting to solve your problems associated with these feelings is a prime way to take charge of the way you'd prefer your life to go.
>
> (Knaus, 2002: 46)

You don't have to be motivated to undertake boring tasks

'I can't get motivated unless I'm under pressure.' This is another example of procrastination based on intolerance of discomfort. This can be called eleventh hour procrastination; you can only get motivated to do the task at the last minute. You have a low threshold for boredom which prevents you from starting these uninteresting tasks earlier. You like the drama and adrenaline rush of living on the edge – cutting it fine and coming through. You believe that this confers on you a heroic image that makes you special, a cut above those around you who attempt to get on with their mundane tasks in a timely fashion. But as Sapadin and Maguire (1996: 171) point out:

> In addition to *weathering* last-minute crises, they [crisis-making procrastinators] are also responsible for *creating* those crises.

Given this fact, how much pride can they genuinely take – and how much real satisfaction can they experience – in getting out of messes they themselves helped to cause? (original italics)

Your behaviour might be applauded or envied by some friends and colleagues. 'How does he do it? That guy's always pulling rabbits out of hats. I'd be worried about leaving things so late before I got stuck into them.' And you often do deliver good work (but overlooking the times when you don't) despite the crisis atmosphere you've created around yourself and which might be inflicted on others such as work colleagues or family members. If the quality of your work does get criticized, you have the ready-made excuse of 'Well it was done at the last minute. I could have done a better job if there had been more time', which also helps to lessen the impact of any self-criticism you may engage in. After the task is finished, you're likely to feel exhausted having worked at warp speed, 'warped and wasted', so to speak. A person who leaves things to the eleventh hour may be surprised to hear that he does, in fact, procrastinate: 'How can I if I get the job done? Procrastinators don't get on with it, I do.'

Jim liked to use phrases such as 'coming in on a wing and a prayer' and 'slipping in under the wire' to indicate his prowess at getting projects in on time using minimal time to complete them, though he tended to conveniently forget his colleagues' frustrations that his tardiness was interfering with the completion of their own work. When he worked from home, he could only get going late at night – his day was filled with inactivity or doing more pleasurable things – and often worked through the night, sometimes disrupting the sleep of his family. The next day he would go to work tired but triumphant with a 'Done it again'. However, Jim was aware that he wasn't always happy with his approach to task completion:

JIM: Though I like the rush when I'm coming up to the wire, there is a lot of strain and tiredness in doing what I do. I sort of get into a boom and bust way of operating.

MICHAEL: Would you teach your children to work in that way?

JIM: No. I want them to approach things in a steady, methodical way. Start their homework earlier. Definitely not to leave it just before bedtime or just before they go to school.

MICHAEL: What stops you from starting your work earlier?

JIM: I have tried but I get so awfully bored. I'm not in the mood, I don't feel motivated. How are you supposed to work on something if you are not motivated?

MICHAEL: Have you considered the possibility that you don't have to be motivated to start and continue working, that motivation may come later, but you won't find that out until you try it?

JIM: What if the motivation doesn't come despite keeping on with it?

MICHAEL: What do you say to your children when they complain about having to do their boring homework when they don't want to do it?

JIM: [sheepishly] Well, you've just got to get on with it. Okay, I can see where this is leading.

MICHAEL: [tapping my forehead] Do you know what your belief is that stops you from tolerating the boredom of starting your work much earlier in an unmotivated state?

JIM: Well, I said I get bored.

MICHAEL: You can be bored but still continue to work on a task.

JIM: [musing] Why should I do something I don't want to do? I don't want to do it and I don't! I get on with something more interesting [laughing]. I sound like a spoilt child. All right, I know deep down I do want to do something about it. That's why I've come to see you.

MICHAEL: Good. You know, as well as your aversion to boredom, your boom and bust approach severely restricts the range of options you could give yourself in approaching your work.

JIM: What do you mean?

MICHAEL: For example, starting tasks, particularly the important ones, much earlier gives you that steady and methodical way of working that you say you want for your children. Starting earlier gives you more time to review your work in order to improve it and spot errors. At present, you give yourself precious little time, if any, to review it. And you don't give yourself the chance to raise your frustration tolerance level so that you can work while feeling bored and uncomfortable; instead, you flee from boredom. You believe you can only work when the pressure really starts to build which deprives you of the choice of starting and finishing earlier so you can approach the deadline in a relaxed rather than a frantic state. That's what I mean by restricting your options.

JIM: Okay, I'm convinced, but I'm not happy about starting earlier.

MICHAEL: You don't have to be happy about it but is it in your
    longer term interests to do it?

JIM: It is. Okay, in for a penny, in for a pound. I'd better get started
    then.

The image of approaching a deadline in a relaxed state reminds
me of a story told by a leading cognitive behavioural therapist, the
late Albert Ellis, who said that when he was studying at university
he would start an essay as soon as he got it. He noticed, to his
delight, that the books he needed to use for his essay would be
there on the library shelves. Once he finished the essay he could
take it relatively easy for the rest of the term. Most of the other
students preferred to enjoy themselves rather than knuckle down
immediately and so put off tackling the essay until the deadline
loomed when there would be fierce competition for the books
and much frustration for those who couldn't get their hands on
them, thereby igniting fears that they would receive lower marks
for their essays.

Jim forced himself into beginning uninteresting tasks much
earlier and working on them in a steady and consistent way. This
was a very unnatural state for Jim to experience and he complained
that 'this isn't me'. This apparent loss of identity can interfere
with the process of change or stop it. Giving up familiar but self-
defeating thoughts, feelings and behaviours can feel 'strange' or
'unnatural' as you work towards acquiring a more productive
problem-solving outlook. This dissonant state created by the clash
or tension between new and old ways of doing things can lead you
to give up trying to change in order to become 'natural' again
(Neenan and Dryden, 2002b). If you persist in tolerating this
dissonant state, you're likely to see the new emerging changes as
more familiar now and some of the old behaviours as somewhat
strange and, consequently, they have less of a hold on you.

Jim thought he was turning into a boring person because he was
doing boring tasks in a boringly unfamiliar 'not in the nick of time'
way. How boring was that? Doing boring tasks does not make you
a boring person, no matter how strongly you believe it. As I
mentioned in the section on self-acceptance in Chapter 5 (p. 76),
you're made up of many aspects and to pick one, no matter how
big it seems, can never capture the complexity of you as a person.
Jim said he would try to stop defining himself so narrowly as
'boring' and persist with tolerating his dissonant state.

Creativity can be injected into boring tasks, a playfulness to lighten your mood. Jim liked the sound of that. He enjoyed going to fancy dress parties, so he decided to dress up as someone famous (e.g. Abraham Lincoln or Groucho Marx) when he was working on a project at home. This gave him the stimulus to get going. He eventually phased out dressing up when he could get himself going under his own steam, but kept this playfulness aspect of task completion in reserve in case it might be needed when the work seemed 'too dreary'. He also started meditation classes as he needed to learn to relax in order to reduce the level of self-created drama in his life.

There remained the issue of Jim's pursuit of the adrenaline rush. This pursuit had self-defeating consequences when applied to his work, so he sought activities such as parachuting and skiing to give him this excitement without the accompanying crises he usually experienced 'living on the edge' (Sapadin and Maguire, 1996). The overall quality of his work improved, a calmer atmosphere prevailed at home and he made himself more of a team player at work.

Rewriting your rules of living to enhance your business performance

Sonya had her own small marketing company advising businesses how best to promote their products and services. When she failed to secure a contract after giving a presentation to a particular business, she tried to shrug it off: 'Win some, lose some. Just move on. It's no failure to experience failure. Successful companies have had their share of failure.' Her mantras didn't help her to cope with failure because she didn't believe the philosophy underpinning them. Even though she won more contracts than she lost, she was unable to shrug off the loss of a contract because, as she said most emphatically, 'They didn't want *me*!' This is another example (and a recurring theme throughout this book) of linking performance to self-worth. Sonya knew she was doing this but didn't know how to stop herself. She put her self-worth on the line at each presentation; she said it was like facing a row of judges and she had to get their approval. A 'thumbs up or down' would determine, in her mind, whether she would return to her office or home in a good or bad mood (if her mood was bad she would complain all evening to her husband about how unfair it was; her sleep would also be adversely affected).

She shuddered at the prospect of doing any cold calling (making unsolicited phone calls to businesses to promote your services) because she would turn it into a 'hot' (emotionally charged) issue if they weren't interested: 'And anyway, it's Sandra's [an employee] job to do the cold calling. I've got more important things to do.' Also, when she spoke about feeling 'gutted' after failing to secure a contract, she emphasized how hard she'd worked on the presentation as if she was entitled to win it simply because of that fact alone: 'If you work hard, then you should be rewarded for it.' She admitted she was an all or nothing thinker on many issues which produced quite marked variations in her mood. She wanted to be more balanced in her thinking, stand on the centre ground: 'I know that's where stability lies, but how do you get there?'

She discussed her upbringing as fraught. She said her mother was always playing her off against her older sister to see who would win her approval. She described her first marriage as 'ghastly'. 'No matter what I did for him it wasn't good enough.' Up until her early thirties, she said her life had been difficult to cope with until she remarried and found happiness for the first time. This gave her the confidence to start her own business after working for a few marketing firms, which showed she had drive and determination. She said her goals were twofold: to build her business by securing contracts with larger companies (business goal); and in therapy to 'get rid of all this soppy poor me stuff. I was watching the *Dragons' Den* [BBC programme] the other night and when the Dragons [leading entrepreneurs] turned down this woman's business idea and she started to cry, I thought that could have been me. I didn't feel sorry for her though. I said to my husband, "She should pull herself together and not take it so personally."' We looked at several areas related to Sonya's 'soppy poor me stuff' in order to help her to develop greater psychological robustness:

1. Making her self-worth conditional on whether she secured the contract

Sonya linked getting the contract to the approval she had sought throughout her life. So she was seeking two contracts: one explicit, based on increasing her business; the other implicit, based on gaining approval to validate her self-worth. I explained the importance of distinguishing between never rating yourself and only rating aspects of yourself (e.g. a relationship fails and you want to find another one, but you're not a failure because of it; you dislike your impulsiveness and try to curb it, but refuse to condemn yourself for it). She found this explanation difficult to understand (many clients do) and wanted a visual way of understanding the concept. I produced a packet of peanuts (this technique is adapted from Wessler and Wessler, 1980).

MICHAEL: This packet contains peanuts that taste great, horrible and just okay. Is the packet great, horrible or just okay based on its contents?

SONYA: It's just a packet.

MICHAEL: Okay. Just say all the peanuts were horrible. Would that make the packet horrible?

SONYA: It's still just a packet.

MICHAEL: If the peanuts were all great, would that make the packet great?

SONYA: It's still just a packet. I sound like a parrot.

MICHAEL: What about if I tipped out the peanuts and replaced them with diamonds, pebbles and bits of chocolate? What would you say now?

SONYA: Wonderful. Give me the packet!

MICHAEL: Does the 'wonderful' refer to the packet or its contents?

SONYA: The contents, just the diamonds, and before you ask me, it's not a wonderful packet, just a packet.

The crucial point is to focus on the content of the packet (aspects of the self), not on the packet (self). In other words, stop rating the self, but rate only aspects of the self. Some of these aspects change over time (replacing the peanuts with diamonds, pebbles and chocolate), so it is pointless to think that a single global label (e.g. 'I'm a failure') can define for ever the complexity and changeability of a person. She could see the sense in this concept and would keep a packet of peanuts on her desk at work to remind her of this crucial separation to make in evaluating what happens to her in life. In her words – 'It's not about *me*!' Making your self-worth unconditional can be very hard to absorb into your outlook, but worth striving to do as you are less likely to allow yourself to be sidetracked into self-condemnation when things go wrong and, instead, focus your energies on trying to put things right or accepting what cannot be changed.

2. Tackling her sense of entitlement

Sonya believed that she should not only get the contract because of the effort she put into preparing and giving the presentation but also was entitled to it as compensation for her hard life. Would she say this to the executives she stood before? 'Of course not. I know it's ridiculous.' They would be interested in only what she could do for their business and would not want to waste their time listening to her sob stories. She realized she was playing the role of a victim which she didn't like. To convince herself both in her head as well as her heart that it was 'ridiculous', she needed to think strategically. 'How do I want to be in my business dealings three or six months from now, if not sooner?' Instead of reacting like a victim and remaining 'committed to protest of the past . . . From the perspective of the proactive strategic individual, the world is neither just nor unjust – it simply *is what it is*' (Leahy, 2001: 163; original italics). For Sonya, her strategic thinking meant removing all surplus meaning (i.e. thinking like a victim) from contract negotiations or presentations and focusing only on what she needed to do to make the best business case for her company to be chosen and accepting, without despair, when it wasn't.

3. Marked variations in her mood

These were related to her conditional self-acceptance. Your assumptions, often stated in an 'if . . . then' form, about how events should or should not turn out can determine whether your mood goes up or down (Fennell, 1999). In Sonya's case, 'If I get the contract, then this means I'm a worthwhile person' (high mood, temporary until the next setback) and 'If I don't get the contract, this means I'm no good' (low mood, her negative self-belief has been confirmed). These assumptions were stated in all or nothing terms that 'I keep on doing'. Using the strategies discussed in 1 and 2 above, she was able to achieve much longer periods of mood stability through developing balanced thinking – the middle ground where she wanted to get to.

4. Learning from failure

Sonya had really wanted to believe this but couldn't see the learning until she stopped personalizing failure ('If you fail at something, then you're a failure as a person'). Kottler (2001) suggests the following benefits to be derived from failure:

(a) promotes reflection on what you are doing and how you could do it better
(b) stimulates change by discovering new problem-solving approaches
(c) provides feedback on what went wrong
(d) encourages flexibility to think beyond your current ways of doing things
(e) improves your frustration tolerance for dealing with situations that don't turn out the way you expected
(f) teaches humility about the limitations of your knowledge and abilities, pricking the bubble of arrogant self-assurance.

Sonya wanted her business to 'step up', i.e. secure contracts with larger companies. She eventually gained her first opportunity to make a presentation to a larger company. She didn't get the contract but the feedback offered was that her presentation was excellent. Her lack of experience in working with larger companies was the telling factor. She was both disappointed and excited by what had happened: 'Obviously I wanted to get it, but I didn't get into that failure and victim nonsense routine. I saw it as strictly business, I really did. I'm so pleased with how I responded to it. My husband was very surprised that I didn't spend all evening moaning about it as I would have done in the past. I'm going to persist with trying to step up.'

Don't use a vocabulary of catastrophe to make a difficult situation worse than it actually is

Attending an interview can be a sleep-depriving, stomach-shrinking, nerve-shredding experience if you see yourself drying up, talking gibberish, asking idiotic questions, freezing, running out of the room, shaking uncontrollably and a host of other imagined 'horrors'; in essence, making a complete fool of yourself. I use inverted commas to indicate that these 'horrors' are self-created rather than reflect objectively the circumstances you face. Can you equate the 'horror' of talking gibberish in an interview with the genuine horror of watching your child being tortured?

Myra's interview fear was freezing and she used a vocabulary of catastrophe to describe it: 'Oh my God . . . it's terrible . . . nothing could be worse . . . it's unbearable.' Myra believed that it was the interview itself that made her freeze rather than anything she might be doing. She had experienced episodes of freezing but was usually nudged out of them by the interviewer asking, 'Are you all right?' She had been doing deep relaxation exercises, learning abdominal breathing to counteract her rapid and shallow breathing when feeling tense, and practising interview techniques (e.g. sitting upright, making eye contact, not giving waffling replies to questions, seeking clarification when she didn't understand something) in simulated interview situations, all designed to reduce her high anxiety levels which she hoped would stop her freezing. What she had not been doing was targeting for challenge and change the catastrophic thoughts and images that turned an unpleasant, but not dangerous, experience into a perceived nightmare.

Myra's belief that 'interviews make me freeze' is an example of what I described in Chapter 2 as A→C thinking, i.e. it's situations that make you react in the way that you do, and contrasted this with B→C thinking, i.e. that your thinking largely determines how you react to situations. To orient her to B→C thinking, and with her agreement, I suggested the nickname 'Myra the Magnifier' to show her how, through her use of language, she was adding psychological disturbance to an unpleasant experience (e.g. 'It's unbearable to feel like this at interviews'), and to remove these apocalyptic words and phrases from her vocabulary. She was prone to such usage in other areas of her life such as being stuck in traffic jams or long queues in shops. In other words, she needed to keep a sense of perspective.

I encouraged her to do an imagery exercise twice daily for several weeks where she imagined herself beginning to freeze in an interview – she would get very tense while doing this – and then talk to herself in a moderate and calming way, including asking the interview panel for a few moments to compose herself, in order to take the 'horror' out of the situation and thereby see herself unfreezing to continue the interview. To do imagery exercises where the freezing does not occur would be avoiding the very fears she needed to address. Regular exposure to this initially frightening situation helped her to see that she could manage herself effectively in an interview. Through regular practice, some clients are able to make themselves bored with their self-created 'horrors' and give them up. At the next interview, Myra, though 'tense and uptight', guided herself reasonably well through it: 'There were moments when I felt the freezing up beginning but the imagery practice helped me not to get catastrophic about it.' She didn't get the job, but 'I was pleased with the outcome anyway'.

Resilience at work

Whatever the challenges you face in the workplace, it's important to find an inner stability that helps you not to feel overwhelmed or 'stressed out' by these challenges. When I worked in the NHS there was always some change afoot and I found it helpful not to allow myself to get sucked into all the rumours and gossip circulating around the department, but instead to wait for the changes to be formally announced and then decide how best to absorb them into my daily work routine. Dwelling on the rumours added nothing of value or clarity to my work.

If your attention is always externally focused, it can be easy to blame others or events for your stress and therefore not consider the contribution that you're making to it. Looking inwards helps you to locate the attitudes that interfere with your ability to adapt to changing circumstances. Change will be imposed upon you whether you welcome it or not and encountering difficulties in your career is unavoidable, but you retain the choice of how you respond to these events. In the next chapter, I look at how a resilient mindset can be used in relationships.

Chapter 7

Resilience in relationships

Introduction

> Relationships are potentially very satisfying, they protect us
> from loneliness and improve our physical and mental health. A
> two-parent family is also the most successful setting for the
> care and upbringing of children.
>
> (Crowe, 2005: 3)

I know I'm stating the obvious when I say that relationships can
also be hard work and this is why resilience is required in finding,
building, maintaining, repairing or ending them. Some couples are
bewildered, angry and/or saddened by how they could be so much
in love at one time yet now can hardly stand the sight of each
other. I once saw a couple who, even though they still lived
together, came to the first session in separate cars, refused to come
into my office together unless there was a gap of a minute between
each other's entry (this was negotiated on their mobile phones), sat
as far apart as possible, and hurled insults at each other as soon as
we started. As I was telling them the ground rules for couples
counselling such as putting their respective viewpoints without
insulting or threatening each other in the process, one of them
asserted, 'It's pointless anyway' and walked out. The other partner
said, 'See what I've got to put up with?' and then also left. The
session was over in less than 15 minutes. Their relationship was
well past the point of no return and heaven knows what they
thought I could do for them. Maybe they imagined I could supply
some 'magic bullet' technique or insight that would pull them back
from the brink of separation even though they had long been
separate in every way apart from living under the same roof.

Relationship difficulties of one kind or another make up a considerable proportion of my caseload. With regard to difficulties between couples, many unhappy partners come on their own to see me as the other partner, for whatever reason, does not wish to attend. Instead of the preferred couples counselling I would like to undertake, therapy focuses on the person's unilateral attempts to improve the relationship in her favour by satisfying some of her interests and desires. Her unilateral actions may result in one or more of the following outcomes: achieving the changes she wants to see; encouraging her partner to come to therapy to present his side of the case and then couples counselling can commence (if he believes I can be neutral after having been an advocate for his partner's interests); giving up trying to improve the relationship in the face of his refusal to budge on any issue and reverting to resentful passivity; looking for satisfaction outside of the relationship; or deciding to leave the relationship because of his unwillingness to compromise.

Friendships can follow a similar path of falling out, making up or calling it a day, though I've never encountered friends who've come to therapy to work out their troubled relationship. Relationships can cover a wide range of people you're involved with, such as parents, children, relatives, work colleagues, neighbours, but in this chapter my focus will be limited to couples and friends.

Don't turn rejection by others into self-rejection

When looking for a partner it's important to have a thick skin to cope with the expected rejections, not to take the whole business too seriously, to collect some stories to amuse your friends with and embark upon partner seeking in a spirit of curiosity rather than viewing it as a nerve-wracking experience which will tell you whether you're still desirable. Emma was in her early fifties, had been married twice and was on the lookout for a third husband. She decided on internet dating. She arranged to meet the men in pubs, restaurants or bars. She said that these dates ended in one of two ways: either he would say at some point that he's just going to the toilet but didn't come back, or if he stayed till the end of the evening, promised to phone her but never did. She said the final indignity was arranging to meet a man in a bar who, when he walked in, looked her up and down, smiled and then walked out: 'He was gone before I'd finished introducing myself. It was terrible.' When I met Emma she wanted me to help her find out what was wrong with her – illuminate her heart of darkness to discover the terrible truth about herself – which was what I didn't do.

MICHAEL: Why should there be anything wrong with you?

EMMA: Well, they don't come back and that last one . . .

MICHAEL: But why should they come back if they don't fancy you?

EMMA: Well, it must mean I'm unattractive, lost my looks or something worse. I want them to come back.

MICHAEL: You may be unattractive to them, but that doesn't mean *you're* unattractive. If they come back you're attractive and if they don't come back you're unattractive. How can your looks change so quickly?

EMMA: I know it sounds silly but why don't they come back then?

MICHAEL: I don't know. Are you going to send each one a questionnaire to find out, and if they did send them back, what would you do with their answers?

EMMA: I probably wouldn't read them. Don't want to hear the truth.

MICHAEL: But what truth are you talking about? So far, six men haven't fancied you and you're jumping to gruesome conclusions about yourself. Did you fancy all six?

EMMA: No, only one looked promising.

MICHAEL: So even the five you didn't fancy have to show an interest in you to prove you're attractive. Is that right?

EMMA: I suppose so. I'm being pathetic about all this.

MICHAEL: How could you be tougher about it then if you're going to continue internet dating?

EMMA: A couple of friends of mine are doing the same thing as me but they see it as a giggle, take it all sort of casual.

MICHAEL: Presumably they don't waste time on tormenting themselves about their supposed faults and failings like you do.

EMMA: That's right, they don't. If a bloke is not interested in them, they move on to the next one.

MICHAEL: Could you take a leaf or two out of their book to make this business of looking for a husband reasonably light-hearted rather than allowing it to be weighed down with deadly seriousness and fault finding?

EMMA: Remind myself that I will eventually find Mr Right.

MICHAEL: Before you find Mr Right, how do you want to cope with the rejections?

EMMA: I don't know. I'm stuck.

MICHAEL: On what?

EMMA: The usual thing: if they don't fancy me, then there must be something wrong with me.

MICHAEL: Any ideas how to break this connection?

EMMA: What if I did it literally?

MICHAEL: Can you explain?

EMMA: Well, write down on a card, 'If they don't fancy me, then there must be something wrong with me', and tear it in half before I go out on a date to remind myself to break the connection. I'd throw away the 'something wrong with me' bit.

MICHAEL: So you'll keep the part that reads 'If they don't fancy me . . .', but that still needs an answer.

EMMA: I'll write, 'So what!' That's what my friend says and it works for her. Do you think it'll work for me?

MICHAEL: We don't know at this stage. That's the whole point of an experiment: to see what happens. What's the attitude that lies behind 'So what!'?

EMMA: Not to take dating too seriously as if it's a life or death thing. See it as a bit of fun.

MICHAEL: Okay. Good luck.

EMMA: I'll need it.

Emma battled her way through more dates and rejections as well as turning down men whose interest in her wasn't reciprocated. This showed, she agreed, that she still had 'pulling power'. When she had been on dates with men she found attractive, the relationships fizzled out: 'One was so controlling, texting me all the time to find out what I was doing and who I was with. It got very creepy, so he had to go. Then there was another one who never stopped talking about himself. You'd think I wasn't there! He had to go too. They're not what they appear to be when you first meet them.'

With all the stories she told me in our sessions, it was very obvious that she had turned herself into a hardened veteran of the 'dating game'. Rejection by others didn't lead any longer to self-rejection, just the few odd moments of self-doubt – 'Those two words "So what!" keep reminding me not to put myself down' – and she was also dishing out the rejections herself: 'I met this bloke for a drink and within half an hour I was screaming to get out of there. He was so boring. Previously, I would have stayed all evening to be polite but I told him I wasn't interested and left. Can you imagine me doing that when I first came here?' By the end of therapy she still hadn't met Mr Right but was ploughing on nevertheless. Eighteen months later she sent me a letter enclosing a photograph of husband number three. She had got tired of dating and decided to 'have a rest'. It was while she was 'resting' that she met him at a local church event.

Re-establishing caring communication

Couples counselling is a balancing act for the therapist: I have to strive to give each person equal time to put their case and not be seen to take sides and at the same time prevent the session from degenerating into pointless bickering (repeating in the session what they do at home) by providing a structure to follow. If they're motivated to stay together, then what constructive actions are they both going to engage in to repair their fractured relationship? Beck (1988: 5) suggests that distressed couples need help with 'correcting their misinterpretations, untying the knots that twisted their communication, and tuning up their abilities to see and hear their partners' signals accurately'. Instead of sniping at each other from familiar positions, they need to put down their weapons and jointly resolve to work out their problems in a spirit of negotiation and with clear communication guiding the way. Communication between warring couples is usually heavily laden with the negative meanings that each infers from what the other has said or done. For example, Joy and Barry, two young hard-working profes- sionals, couldn't have a conversation without it escalating into 'What's the point?' frustration on both sides:

JOY: Anything wrong? You haven't spoken for a while.
['Have I done something to upset him?']
BARRY: There's nothing wrong. I'm just thinking.
['She's always prying into my business.']
JOY: You look like you're in a bad mood. Have I done something?
['Why won't he talk to me? Has he found someone else?']
BARRY: It's nothing to do with you.
['Why does everything that happens to me have to involve her?']
JOY: Well don't tell me then! [Stalks off.]
['He's pathetic, sulking like a drama queen.']

BARRY: I wasn't planning to! [Hurls a book across the room.]
['Why does she always behave like that? She's infuriating.']

In the session, such couples usually have lots of examples, ready to be unleashed, illustrating the injustices, grievances, hurts inflicted on them by their partner. Hearing all this would be destructive to repairing the relationship (therapy would resemble an endless slanging match), so I usually ask each partner to select one or two key examples that pinpoint for them what's wrong with the relationship. This is an exercise in listening to understand instead of listening to respond: if the person is engaged in the former kind of listening he genuinely wants to see the situation from his partner's viewpoint, while if it's the latter kind he's impatient for his partner to stop talking – he's not really listening in the first place – in order to put his own side of the story to justify his behaviour in response to hers. Joy said that Barry seemed to avoid intimacy with her such as last weekend when, instead of spending an afternoon with her, he went out on his own knowing she wanted him to stay in. Barry said that when he has a lot on his plate (such as at work at the moment) he likes to be left alone to think and not be burdened with Joy's worries.

At this point, both Joy and Barry were champing at the bit to reply to each other's accusations but I put my hand up to stop them. If the goal was to stay together, which they emphasized it was, what was each prepared to do to address the other's complaints in order to save the relationship – resilient responding to find a constructive way forward, not endless and futile recriminations. So they practised negotiating in the session in clear, empathic language while I was listening for the 'add-ons' that threatened to undermine the negotiations and trigger a fresh round of rows (e.g. 'I would like to spend time with you *if I can fit it in*' or 'If you let me know that you want time alone, that's fine *if you want to be a misery*').

It takes considerable self-restraint and practice to remove these reflexive 'digs' from your language and, instead, focus on problem-solving and relationship-enhancing communication, i.e. a growing emphasis on relational thinking (Epstein, 2004) which moves away from the vicious circle of mutual blame and tit-for-tat behaviour (making the relationship worse) and towards a virtuous circle of looking at each other's behaviour in more benign ways and engaging in positive actions that are likely to be mutually beneficial (improving the relationship). After all, couples presumably want to increase the frequency of positive exchanges between themselves and decrease the frequency of negative ones and re-engage in jointly shared and enjoyed activities that may have stopped or are now few in number (Epstein, 2004). Two people living together but the relationship – an intimate bond – is missing and needs to be rediscovered.

Joy and Barry did their best to try and remember the distinction between listening to understand and listening to respond in finding solutions to their problems. Often they were like two lawyers haggling over the small print in drawing up a contract. For example, Joy agreed to go swimming with Barry but he wanted to do his usual 60 lengths as part of his fitness programme while she wanted to 'splash around' with him: 'We're supposed to be doing something together yet he wants to be on his own again.' So they agreed to spend more time splashing around together before he went off to do a reduced number of lengths. Another example: Barry said he took an interest in some of Joy's hobbies but not all of them: 'She likes collecting fine china. The subject bores me. Why should I pretend to be interested in it when I'm not?' Joy thought that if he wasn't interested in all of her interests this meant he didn't care about her. Joy accepted this was an unrealistic belief to hold but agreed 'as long as he shows some interest in some of my interests'. This negotiation in specific situations reflected the wider struggle in the relationship over time and its meaning. For Joy, as much time together as possible meant a close and loving relationship while Barry, though keen to rebuild a closer relationship, also wanted to maintain some independence in the relationship by having his own time, more than Joy was happy with.

Though they would occasionally row over these issues and all the old grievances would put in an appearance, I pointed out it was essential to keep their goal in mind and keep tracking their progress towards achieving it. In my office, I had written in big letters on the flipchart, WE WANT TO STAY TOGETHER HAPPILY, and if they started to argue I would point to the flipchart which was enough to stop them, they would apologize to each other and then restart negotiations to overcome their stuck points. Compromise is essential if you want a relationship to survive. This indicates that both individuals are striving for equality rather than seeing the relationship as a power struggle where there is a fight to gain the upper hand and keep it. One partner's strength is drawn

from the weaknesses of the other or by exploiting their vulnerabilities (this power imbalance is often reversed when the weaker/
exploited partner finally rises up).

Joy and Barry settled their disagreements and said their relationship was now in a 'state of relative harmony – we're still going
to have our ups and downs'. Through therapy, they were now much
more accepting of each other's idiosyncrasies (the other partner's
perceived peculiarities) which is a key ingredient in a relationship if
love is to endure (Hauck, 1981a). In the later stages of therapy, they
would hold hands in the session (not something couples usually
engage in at the beginning of therapy). We looked at what they
would need to do on a lifelong basis (basically, keep practising the
skills they had learnt) if they wanted to maintain their gains from
therapy and not to expect these gains to stay in place automatically.
Follow-up appointments were agreed to monitor their progress.

Couples counselling is often complex and I've only scratched the
surface in this section, but fundamentally if there is no real commitment to save the relationship, I can't save it for them and
attention can then turn to the possibility of separating amicably
which also requires a resilient response, i.e. accepting with sadness
but not bitterness that the relationship is over, stopping feuding,
and negotiating the division of joint assets, maintenance payments
and access to the children in a fair and impartial way or as near as
you can get to it.

Standing up for yourself in order to make constructive changes in your life

Let sleeping dogs lie may be a piece of advice offered to you by
others but if you're not prepared to follow it, are you ready for the
consequences of waking them up? This was the question Jill
pondered. Her marriage was going through a rough patch 'where
my husband does a lot of inconsiderate things and, taken together,
I wonder if he still wants to be with me'. Why didn't she speak up
when he acted inconsiderately? She said she wasn't sure but would
feel anxious if she did, so we took one example (her husband
snatching from her the remote control for the television) to 'drill
down' to her underlying beliefs using the downward arrow technique (Burns, 1999) which I described in Chapter 6 (p. 100). This
technique follows the personal meaning of each revealed thought in
order to discover, in this case, the core of Jill's anxiety. I started by

asking her what was anxiety provoking in her mind if she challenged his behaviour regarding the remote control:

> 'He might get angry with me.'
> ↓   'And if he did?'
> 'He might not speak to me.'
> ↓   'And if he didn't speak to you?'
> 'He might get fed up with me and find someone else.'
> ↓   'Let's suppose he finds someone else.'
> 'Then I'll be all alone.'
> ↓   'What would that mean to you?'
> 'It would be unbearable.'
> ↓   'What would make it unbearable?'
> 'I can't cope on my own. I'd go to pieces.'
> ↓   'Is that what you are most anxious about?'
> 'Yes. I can't cope on my own.'

Now it was clear to Jill why she didn't speak up. Silence protected her from experiencing these feared consequences. Yet she was fed up with being on the receiving end of his inconsiderate behaviour and angry with herself for being unassertive: 'If I speak up I'll end up alone and fall apart, but if I keep quiet I'll hate myself for it. I'm trapped either way.' Jill had constructed two grim and extreme conclusions about tackling this situation without considering that there could be other viewpoints available to her such as learning to live alone without falling apart, keeping quiet without hating herself for it, speaking up without her husband leaving her or leaving him for someone else if his behaviour didn't improve.

Jill decided to rouse the sleeping dogs but before she got to that point she did some preparatory work on the possibility of living alone in order to remove the 'horror' (emotional disturbance) from it. Looking at the evidence from her past experiences of living alone, she didn't enjoy the experience but there was no 'falling apart'. She realized that what she had done was to equate being unhappy with falling apart. Every day she imagined how she would adapt to living alone in order to make the best of it, she made notes on daily activities she would do including moving from part-time to full-time work, and talked to friends who lived alone and enjoyed it.

When she felt she could make a go of it living alone, she spoke up. When someone starts to change, others have to consider how they're going to respond to these changes. Her husband was surprised by her comments but made no changes in his behaviour. She told me he blamed me for putting these ideas into her head and that things would get back to normal when she stopped therapy. But she persisted with her complaints about his behaviour. Her husband now upped the stakes by telling her he was moving out because 'he couldn't stand my nagging any more', hoping this would bring the matter to an end by Jill backing down (we had previously discussed the likelihood of her husband using this tactic and whether she would call his bluff at this point). She wavered for a day or two, then increased the stakes herself by packing his bags and leaving them by the front door. 'I felt very nervous about what I was doing yet could feel myself getting stronger at the same time. I was now determined to play it out, to the bitter end if necessary.' Her husband left, but returned several days later ready to talk and make changes in his behaviour. She said he seemed very glad to be back. While she was relieved that they were going to stay together, a power shift had occurred in the relationship whereby 'He's now wary about doing something I might not like in case *I walk out on him*; in fact, he now seems to need me more than I need him. I don't want to be a domineering bitch or anything like that, but he knows what I won't put up with and that's the important thing. Looking back, I'm glad I woke those dogs up.'

Keeping cool when provoked

Paul's divorce was bitter and expensive and there were times when he and his wife would only talk to each other through their lawyers. He had access to his two children, mainly at the weekends, and wanted to be involved as much as possible in decision making about their welfare. He would be seeing his ex-wife for a long time to come and therefore wanted to achieve a post-divorce 'peace treaty' with her: 'But when I go round there to pick them up or I speak to her on the phone or she cancels me coming at the last minute because she's got other plans for the children that weekend, I see red. I want to be reasonable. I try to keep my cool every time she makes a cutting comment about me and keep to the business at hand, but I can't seem to do it and we end up arguing.'

What stopped him from keeping his cool? When clients say that they want to be cool or calm in the face of some adversity or difficulty they're really focusing on the wrong goal at this stage.

Feeling calm or cool comes later. The real question is: What stops you from being cool or calm in the first place? That is the focus of clinical attention. I asked him for a recent example when he was unable to keep his cool. He said he went to his wife's house to pick up the children and she told him to wait in the car while she brought them out because her new partner was there and then added, 'At last I've found a real man.' This last comment triggered a testy exchange between them. He said his wife had made derogatory comments about his sexual prowess when their relationship was going from bad to worse. He felt he had to defend himself but, at a deeper level, wondered if she was right because she had a higher sex drive than he did which he couldn't keep up with and maybe, after all, he was less of a man.

He said that when he was younger a lot of his male friends were 'heavy drinkers and womanizers, activities I wasn't that keen on and they used to take the mickey out of me because I didn't indulge as much as they did. So I used to worry if there was something wrong with me because I wasn't up for it all the time like my mates seemed to be'. These doubts about his manliness pre-dated his marriage, so his ex-wife's comments reinforced his doubts, she did not put them there. I pointed out that having a lower sex drive didn't make him less of a man unless he thought so, which he appeared to do. All the examples he described revolved around his masculinity: 'She said she hoped our son wouldn't grow up to be as spineless as me. Is she right?' He was judging himself through his wife's eyes, reinforced by his own longstanding doubts, and the 'verdict' was always the same: he was inadequate in some way.

If he really wanted to learn to keep his cool when he spoke to his ex-wife and attend to the business at hand (i.e. the children), then he would need to make up his own mind about himself and his life and stop seeing himself through his wife's eyes as if this was the 'truth' about him. This wasn't easy to do as he would often start a sentence with 'Well, she thinks . . .' and I would have to interrupt and remind him that the question was what he thought and how he wanted to see himself. We also practised dealing with his ex-wife's caustic comments through, initially, me modelling how to respond to such comments without making himself upset over them (e.g. 'It's true you have a higher sex drive than me and I used to think there was something wrong with me for not being able to match it. Now I realize that my sexual requirements are very different from yours which is one of the reasons we broke up.'). With his permission, I would say unpleasant things to him to see how well he responded. When he faltered in his replies, we would examine the stuck points which usually meant he had slipped back to seeing himself in derogatory terms (e.g. 'She used to tell me that when we argued I should have stood up to her more, told her to shut up . . . in other words, be more of a man.').

Paul worked hard to redefine masculinity in his terms (e.g. sensitive, quiet, conscientious, moderate sex drive, a good father) rather than adopt the views of others on this subject. From his new perspective on masculinity, he was able eventually to defuse my unpleasant comments and respond in an equable way: 'I don't want to dignify your comments with a reply.' He said his aim was to keep silent if his ex-wife made any derogatory comments about him and only respond to issues regarding his children.

He realized this would be difficult but as I pointed out in Chapter 1, acting resiliently can be seen as a ratio between helpful and unhelpful behaviour in pursuit of your goals (e.g. engaging in helpful behaviour 75 per cent of the time and engaging in unhelpful behaviour 25 per cent of the time). So resilience does involve acting non-resiliently at times, but it's important to ensure that your resilience balance sheet shows more assets (occurrences of helpful behaviour) than liabilities (occurrences of unhelpful behaviour). Sometimes Paul did snap back at his ex-wife when he thought she was making derogatory comments about him, but over time the occasions when this occurred dropped considerably and his resilience balance sheet showed many more assets than liabilities: 'The less I respond, the less she does it.' He said that the testy exchanges between them continued to fade away and a 'sort of peace treaty finally prevailed'.

Fallible people can be the best of friends

Friendships can be as troubling as romantic relationships. Dominique said her friend Gemma was 'great in every way except her lousy timekeeping which makes me so angry. She says I'm a great friend to her, so she should bloody well sort out the lateness thing and then the relationship would be really great!' Dominique had asked some of her other friends for their views and the consensus was that she should stop seeing Gemma if she made herself that upset over her lateness and Gemma wasn't prepared to change her behaviour. She had spoken to Gemma about it, 'But all she says is that she can't help it and she'll try harder.' Dominique said she got so angry about Gemma's lateness that 'I sometimes feel on the brink of ending the friendship in a great destructive outburst but I always pull back from the brink because I want to keep seeing her because, after all, she's still a great friend.' She said there must be other options open to her in dealing with this issue but she couldn't see what they might be. As I've said elsewhere in this book, before you attempt to influence someone else's behaviour, manage your own behaviour first because that's within your ability to change.

Dominique was making herself angry by demanding that Gemma be what she obviously wasn't, i.e. punctual. Like Raymond, the first client presented in the previous chapter, Dominique was banging her head against her internally constructed brick wall. This is how Gemma must behave in order to satisfy Dominque's vision of the 'really great' friendship. But Gemma, for whatever reason, wasn't prepared to make the effort to be punctual. As Dominique didn't want to end the relationship or issue ultimatums, she would need to accept, not mentally rail against, Gemma's lateness if she wanted to reduce the intensity of her anger. Also, she would need to focus on the relationship as a whole rather than overly focus on the lateness (looking at the relationship through the lens of the lateness made the relationship seem at times much less satisfying than it actually was). A relationship can be 'really great' despite the fallible (imperfect) behaviour of its participants. Did she want a flawless Gemma (the fantasy) or a great but flawed Gemma (the reality)? She said, in truth, the flawless Gemma, and that's why, I observed, she was stuck in her anger. This last point really resonated with Dominique and she later described it as 'not seeing the beam in my own eye because I'm focused on the mote in Gemma's eye', i.e. the fault was greater in herself than the person she was finding fault with. With her anger moderated, she was able to move into practical problem solving. We used the ADAPT model of problem solving (Nezu et al., 2007) which I described in Chapter 5 (pp. 86–87).

A = **attitude** (positive): 'This problem can be sorted out as I'm now focused on the beam in my own eye.'
D = **defining the problem and setting realistic goals**: 'My problem up to now was the rigidity in my thinking about how Gemma must be which meant she was always falling short of my ideal. My goal is to accept Gemma's lateness as part of the really great friendship we have.'

A = generating alternative solutions: 'So, what options do I have in my attempt to achieve my goal? I could (writing them down):

1   Tell Gemma what's been troubling me [Dominique hadn't revealed the true extent of her feelings].
2   My acceptance strategy doesn't mean I can't ask her to improve her timekeeping.
3   Plan things to take into account her lateness such as telling her the table at the restaurant is booked for 8.30 when actually it's for 9.
4   Try to get to the bottom of her lateness to help me understand what's going on.
5   Just forget all about the lateness.
6   Remind myself that accepting her lateness doesn't mean I like it but I'm not going to upset myself over it either. That's all I can think of at the present time.'

P = predicting the consequences and developing a solution plan: 'What are the likely consequences for each alternative solution in helping me to reach my goal? Let me see:

1   I will do this one but without blaming her for my anger. It will help me to be honest about my feelings.
2   I'll keep mentioning this as there are small improvements from time to time before she slips back.
3   Definitely do this which will help me adjust to Gemma time.
4   Won't do this. It sounds like I'm still trying to achieve the 'flawless' Gemma by pretending I want to understand her behaviour when, in reality, I'll be pushing her to change it to make me feel happier.
5   No. I'm not going to pretend I don't care about her lateness and thereby live a lie.
6   Yes. I want to keep reminding myself of that in order to maintain a balanced view of her lateness. So my solution plan is to combine options 1, 2, 3 and 6.'

T = trying out the solution to see if it works: 'Well, I did all those things. She was surprised and apologetic when I revealed the extent of my true feelings but there's been no real improvement in her lateness. Now it's something I work around rather than the immovable object I thought, in my wilder moments, would lead me to destroy our friendship. The main point, of course, is that I've adjusted my focus to all the enjoyment I get from the friendship once she's turned up. Shifting my focus has helped me to keep her lateness in perspective rather than letting it dominate my thinking.'

You might think I've missed the most important aspect of the whole story: why was Dominique so angry about Gemma's lateness apart from insisting she should be on time? Did Dominique believe she was being disrespected, or the relationship had to make up for what had been missing in her upbringing and/or other friendships, or having the perfect friend was so tantalizingly close but being denied to her by Gemma's poor timekeeping? We did ponder these and other hypotheses but Dominique usually shrugged her shoulders and said, 'I really don't know'. Pursuing them further was unproductive (I certainly didn't want to put words into her mouth in order to confirm my hypotheses about what was 'really' driving her anger). She was looking for solutions rather than attempting to discover the possible deeper causes for her anger. Sometimes the reason(s) why a problem exists can be unfathomable, but solving it can be relatively straightforward.

Bad behaviour doesn't make a person bad

'When do I stop paying?' This was a question Donovan asked regarding the guilt he continued to feel about a brief affair he had when his marriage was going through a turbulent phase 'and I thought we were going to break up'. He said his wife didn't let him forget the affair, which had occurred several years earlier, and 'brings it up at every opportunity to keep me in line and says how I broke her heart which makes me feel very bad for what I did. She said she doesn't know when or if she could ever forgive me, so I'm stuck in limbo.' Some of you might think he deserves to keep on feeling guilty about betraying his wife's trust and love, but I suggested he could learn how to forgive himself and thereby free himself from his state of psychological servitude (i.e. allowing his wife to maintain her control over him). He didn't have to wait until his wife got round to forgiving him and she might recant later. After all, she could have left him when he told her about the affair, but instead chose to stay (he said she kept on reminding him that he should be grateful she didn't dump him for his act of betrayal).

He thought his wife was using emotional blackmail to keep punishing him (his wife was not interested in coming to therapy to put her side of the story and therefore I had to work with the information he gave me about what was going on). Forward and Frazier (1997: 6) state 'that at the heart of any kind of blackmail is one basic threat, which can be expressed in many different ways: *If you don't behave in the way I want you to, you will suffer*' (original italics). Donovan said his wife knew how to push his 'guilt button' if he didn't give in to her in every dispute, even when he knew he was in the right: 'It's that "haven't you hurt me enough" look that makes me back down.'

So how did he start the process of forgiving himself for the affair? You cannot be emotionally blackmailed unless you allow it to happen. The other person plays on your vulnerabilities thereby creating the impression that she is making you feel guilty about what you did. Your emotions belong to you, not put there magically by someone else, and are largely determined by how you think about what you've done (B→C thinking). If having an affair made you feel guilty (A→C thinking) then every person who had an affair could only ever feel guilty even if they didn't want to – the event would be 'imposing' the feeling on them. Some people have affairs and don't feel guilty about them because, for example, they see them as justifiable if their current relationship is sexually unfulfilling. In Table 2.1 (p. 30) I looked at the themes found in particular emotions; in guilt, the themes are moral lapse and hurting others. Donovan's beliefs reflected these themes: 'I did a bad thing by having an affair which I shouldn't have done. I hurt my wife very badly through betraying her which means I'm a bad person.' By seeing himself as a bad person, it didn't take much effort from his wife to remind him of this 'fact'. If he didn't fall in line with what she wanted, then he thought he was doing more bad things to her: 'That's what a bad person does.'

I explained to him the psychologically healthy alternative to guilt, remorse. A remorseful person accepts that he did a bad thing, but crucially does not condemn himself as a bad person because of it and seeks, but does not beg for, forgiveness from others. Whether or not he receives forgiveness from others, he can forgive himself within the context of compassionate self-acceptance as a fallible (imperfect) human being who while striving to stay on the straight and narrow is not always successful at doing so. The affair may have been a moral lapse, but it was not the whole story of Donovan's life as there was plenty of evidence to show the good things he had done; in other words, his life should be viewed in the round, not just through the narrow perspective of the lapse. This is not letting yourself off the hook because you still have the feeling of remorse to remind you of what you did. Your conscience still pricks you, but not so painfully.

While he could see and accept the difference between guilt and remorse, he still insisted that he hurt his wife very badly and 'it's difficult to forget that'. While he may have contributed significantly to his wife's distress by his unfaithfulness, she ultimately determined the frequency, intensity and duration of the distress she was experiencing. B→C thinking applied as much to her as it did to him. As she chose to stay with him, is this because she wanted to make a go of the relationship or punish him, enjoying the power she exercised over him? It seemed that she wanted to rule him rather than be reconciled with him. Through disentangling what thoughts, feelings and behaviours belonged to him and which ones belonged to his wife, he was able to 'snip' the cognitive wiring attached to his guilt button which meant she was no longer able to manipulate him emotionally by pressing it. Now that he had freed himself from his state of limbo, he could consider his options regarding the marriage in a clear-sighted way.

Rethinking your responsibility for someone else's behaviour

'I'll kill myself if you leave me.' This is an extreme form of emotional blackmail and can be very difficult to deal with if you accept the blackmailer's contention that you would be responsible for his or her death. This scenario can play out in your mind as: 'I leave, he dies, my fault, I suffer never-ending torment.' Janine tried to leave her boyfriend several times, but each time he threatened to take an overdose and each time she reluctantly changed her mind – 'He won't let me go,' she said in despair. More accurately, her feeling of guilt kept her from leaving him.

MICHAEL: How would you be responsible for his death?
JANINE: Because he's made it clear that he will kill himself if I leave, so I have the power of life and death over him.

MICHAEL: The power and responsibility for his life and death belongs to him but, unfortunately, he's pushed it on to you and you've accepted it.

JANINE: I know that's true intellectually but I don't really believe it deeper down.

MICHAEL: What do you really believe deeper down?

JANINE: That I would have killed him by leaving him.

MICHAEL: Could there be any circumstances where he wouldn't kill himself if you left him?

JANINE: Well, if there was another girlfriend lined up to take my place he probably wouldn't do it.

MICHAEL: Any other reasons he might not do it?

JANINE: If he was on speaking terms with his mother, she might then look after him. He hates being on his own.

MICHAEL: So he might decide to act differently if another girlfriend or his mother was on the scene.

JANINE: He might do.

MICHAEL: What about this power you supposedly have over him, is it as powerful as you think if we can find some exceptions when your power over him wouldn't work?

JANINE: I know I don't have this power over him, but I just wish there was another girlfriend standing by then I could leave without feeling guilty.

MICHAEL: You can leave without another girlfriend being ready to take your place when you stop convincing yourself that you would be responsible for his death. When would you be genuinely responsible?

JANINE: If I forced him to take the tablets, literally tipped them down his throat. Obviously I'm not going to do that. I get angry with myself for keep giving in to him all the time. Why can't he stop blackmailing me?

MICHAEL: Why should he? He's getting what he wants and you're giving it to him. Stop seeing your departure and his death as cause and effect. There are a number of ways he can respond to you leaving him and he's chosen – you haven't made him – the suicide option for reasons, highly disturbed reasons, that belong to him and were not put there by you.

JANINE: I've kept on at him to get professional help but he says he doesn't need a psychiatrist, just me. I really wish I could believe I wouldn't be responsible for his death if I left him.

MICHAEL: In order to believe it, you'll need to go over these ideas every day in order to strengthen them in your mind and stop allowing yourself to be brainwashed by him.

JANINE: Okay, just say I left him and he did kill himself, what then? That would be terrible. We did have some good times after all.

MICHAEL: And that would be sad, tragic and it would be healthy to grieve but what might complicate the grieving process is . . .

JANINE: If I blamed myself for his death. I killed him. He would still be alive if I hadn't left him.

MICHAEL: But that's less likely to happen if you can get it crystal clear in your head that he's responsible, not you.

JANINE: That's my struggle.

This clinical dissection of who is ultimately responsible for a person's death is unavoidable in such cases and can seem callous but, as Hauck (1981b) emphasizes, it is even more callous of the person threatening suicide to use it as a means to try and control you, increasing the pressure on you to stay by a suicide attempt if you feel emboldened enough to try and leave, letting you know unequivocally that you made him do it, but then claiming he did it out of love for you. At the end of our sessions, Janine was still psyching herself up to 'cross the Rubicon' as she called it: 'Once I've gone, I won't be coming back under any circumstances.' But that wasn't the end of my involvement with her because she contacted me about a year later to inform me that her former partner had indeed committed suicide after Janine's successor had also left him. What she told me indicated she was 'struggling well' (O'Connell Higgins's [1994] pithy description of resilience). She had obviously summoned up the courage to leave him, felt sad about his death but without any accompanying self-blame for it, and was opening up her life to new possibilities after keeping it on guilt-ridden hold for the last few years.

Don't be complicit in your own exploitation

Rick was in his early twenties, worked as a trader in the City of London and had bought his own house. He had no trouble finding girlfriends and was enjoying the good life. He had lots of exciting plans about how he wanted his career to develop. However (there usually comes a 'however' to darken the bright picture when a client initially tells me what's going right in his life), he worried about what his mates thought about him and seemed to be surprisingly unassertive, given what he told me about his determination in other areas of his life, to speak up about their behaviour towards him. For example, he shared his house with his best friend at 'mates' rates' (relatively low monthly rent) but his best friend was oblivious to Rick's generosity and left the lights on all day, didn't clear up his messes, and invited his friends round and let them stay over without asking Rick's permission: 'I come home from work knackered and I can't relax in my own home. It doesn't feel as if it's my home.' Other examples: when he was down the pub with his friends they would be reluctant to take their turn in buying a round, when taking a taxi they would expect him to pay, and 'I would end up as usual paying the bill in a restaurant'.

This might seem, at first glance, to be his friends exploiting him because he's got a well-paid job (he said all his mates were in work, some of them in jobs as well paid as his). The key point to discover was why he didn't speak up and tell them it's their turn to pay up. He said he would be worried about doing this. We did an ABC example to find out what was at the core of his worry.

> **A = adversity or situation**: imagining telling his mates that it's someone else's turn to buy a round of drinks.
> **B = beliefs**: 'If I do that they'll think I'm a selfish bastard, they won't like me and I'll end up alone, without my mates.'
> **C = consequences**: emotion – worry.

Rick believed that in order to keep his friends from deserting him he had to keep pleasing them, yet he was afraid that they might be talking about him behind his back. He said that when his mates were round his house and he was making coffee and sandwiches for them in the kitchen, he would tiptoe down the hallway and listen outside the room they were sitting in to 'see if they were slagging me off'. He didn't initially see that he was complicit in his own exploitation: in order to keep his friends and avoid the 'horror' of being without them, he was willing to act in a subservient way. When he talked about 'my mates', it was as if he was in thrall to some sort of mystical union that would bind them together for eternity and to oppose it would bring dire consequences to his life: 'We grew up together, went to school together, we get drunk, smoke blow [cannabis], chase women, play football, have a laugh. What's a bloke without his mates?' Because he was transfixed by the all-important concept of mateness, he wasn't assessing each mate to determine whether the relationship should be kept, ended or revised, and he was unable to see himself coping with a life that was mateless (if he got rid of the current crop). This soon changed.

Reflecting on what he got up to with his mates, he said, 'It's just the same old boring shit, sitting around talking about football, lots of late nights, having pizzas delivered all the time, getting drunk. What's so great about that?' He said he was angry with himself for behaving in such a subservient way – 'I like to think I'm in control of my destiny and yet here I am handing it over to others' – and was fired up to get going, but not in a vengeful, payback way. So Rick told his best friend, who rented a room in his house, to pull his weight and also not to invite friends round without his permission; his mates would now have to pay their fair share of the evening's entertainment; and if some of his mates turned up, after the pubs had closed, hoping to continue drinking at his house, he would tell them to go away if he wasn't in the mood for some late-night drinking. All these activities would have been unthinkable just a few months earlier.

Like Louise, the deputy head teacher in the previous chapter, he was amazed at his mates' reaction when he started pushing back: 'I was expecting murders [unpleasant scenes] but, basically, it was, "Alright, why didn't you say so before?" I've stopped being subservient and I'm no longer creeping down the hallway to eavesdrop. In fact, they can say what they like if they wish, I don't really care.' What emerged from our discussions was how limited his expectations of himself were away from his job; so he sought to put that right by doing more things that interested him (e.g. he started training in karate hoping eventually to become a black belt and went on holiday alone to Brazil) and finding new friends and experiences that reflected his changing values.

When he first came to see me, he thought that having to please his friends in order to avoid being seen by them as a 'selfish bastard' was 'hardwired into my brain [he was born with these beliefs]'. However, on closer examination, these beliefs he'd acquired – he wasn't clear how this had happened – could actually be challenged and changed if he was prepared to do some self-examination, risk the possibility of rejection by some or all of his mates by standing up for himself, and re-evaluate the meaning of mateship.

Working at relationships

Most people want to have intimate relationships and friendships – a life is incomplete without them. But with this yearning comes a warning: they can be a lot of trouble. Therefore, it's important to expend the time and effort trying to keep them in good running order through being considerate, not selfish; learning to compromise rather than engaging in competitive struggles to gain the upper hand; communicating clearly and specifically what your dissatisfactions are when you argue and suggesting how they can be resolved without descending into nastiness and hurtful point scoring; accepting the other person's foibles unless they become too pronounced and require constructive and compassionate comment from you (e.g. 'Darling, don't spend too much time daydreaming, we've got to go out in half an hour'); learning to be more appreciative and much less critical in your interactions; and frequently reinvigorating your relationships with mutually enjoyable activities to prevent the vitality in them draining away through unceasing sameness.

If your relationship does come to an end, extract what learning you can from it so there is less chance of repeating the same mistakes in the next one. Just to be free of the relationship may seem like sufficient progress to make but sometimes it is not enough as 'one of the reasons people repeat errors is they fail fully to understand themselves' (Persaud, 2005: 60) and in the next relationship they may find themselves in a similar predicament to the previous one they were so desperate to escape from (e.g. living again with another person who abuses you). Resilience is about becoming psychologically stronger and gaining greater self-understanding through what you've experienced, so take the time to reflect on what you've learnt, write down these lessons and ensure that you can point to enduring changes in your behaviour to demonstrate to yourself that these lessons have indeed been learnt. For example, the next time you get warning signs about a prospective partner's worrying behaviour, act on them instead of overriding them and then you won't have to trouble yourself later with introspective interrogations along the lines of 'How could I have let this happen to me *again*?'

While partners and friends usually put a smile on your face, others individuals can wipe it off. In the next chapter, I look at the resilience required in dealing with people who you believe are making your life difficult for you.

Chapter 8

Resilience in dealing with difficult people

Introduction

In the play *No Exit* by Jean-Paul Sartre (1944/1989), a character remarks that 'Hell is other people' and you may nod in agreement as you conjure up a rogues gallery of people who have made your life exasperatingly difficult, yet never think you could be part of someone else's hell. (As I pointed out in the previous chapter, unhappy couples usually accuse each other of making their lives miserable.) Therefore, when I talk about difficult people, the difficulty with their behaviour is observed from your viewpoint not theirs, unless they admit they are being deliberately difficult in their dealings with you because they enjoy the pleasure of watching you suffer in some way.

With every difficult person you encounter, you will need to examine what aspects of your behaviour may be helping, unintentionally or not, to maintain their oppositional stance towards you. As Siebert (1999) points out, you might see yourself as a person with positive attitudes such as being open-minded and accepting of others yet view with disdain people you perceive as having negative attitudes (e.g. continually fault-finding and complaining). You may not see the irony in your position: for a person with positive attitudes, you have negative attitudes towards people with negative attitudes and thereby engagement with them is likely to be made more difficult than if you had a hopeful attitude that some progress might be made if you're prepared to discuss their viewpoints rather than dismiss them.

Hauck (1998) states that you're at least 51 per cent directly responsible for your own disturbed feelings (e.g. anger, anxiety, depression) by the way you respond to the difficulties and frustrations presented to you by others; these others are no more than 49 per cent indirectly responsible for your emotional difficulties as they don't directly cause them unless they physically attack you, in which case they are 100 per cent responsible. For example, if your partner is constantly unfaithful (his 49 per cent) and is 'making me feel unwanted, undesirable and ill. Why does he keep on behaving like this?', the real questions to ask are: Why are you putting up with his behaviour by staying in the relationship despite your frequent ultimatums to leave, still engaging in sexual relations with him, and linking your desirability to whether or not he is faithful (your 51 per cent)?

You might protest about this 51/49 per cent split and suggest that your contribution is lower (e.g. 20 or 30 per cent) or even nil if you see yourself as the very model of sweet reasonableness and infinite patience and it's the other person driving you round the bend such as your next-door neighbour playing her music too loud. But your very reasonableness and patience which is praised in other situations has not made any impact on encouraging her to reduce the noise level, and you baulk at being assertive with her and spelling out the consequences (e.g. informing the council and/ or police) because you see it as being out of character to behave like that. So your next-door neighbour doesn't turn down the music and you won't adopt different tactics to try and influence her behaviour.

It's important to distinguish between influencing and changing others: you can attempt to influence their behaviour in a positive direction but they make the actual changes – you can't make them – based upon how they are evaluating the situation now. For example, while my son was at school I tried unsuccessfully, and at times angrily, to encourage him to see the importance of doing his homework in a diligent way instead of the reluctant, rushed and haphazard manner he did it in. Now he is at college and has announced that he wants to perform well in his assignments and therefore bends his mind towards doing his homework in a steady, organized and consistent way. It took him a long time to see this and I was unable to accelerate the dawning of this importance while he was at school.

In your dealings with people you perceive to be difficult, first, focus on your own reactions and attitudes to their behaviour and decide what changes are needed in yourself; then turn your focus towards them. When you do focus on them, separate the act(s) from the person, i.e. comment on their behaviour; don't condemn them for their behaviour. As I've said elsewhere in this book, the person is so much larger and more complex than any acts they engage in and to define their worth at any given point (e.g. 'You're an inconsiderate bastard for behaving in that way') not only downgrades them in your mind and maybe reinforces this in their own, but also encourages them to respond in kind and verbal warfare ensues.

Resilience in dealing with difficult people does not mean you will always prevail in influencing them to change. Sometimes you will need to learn to tolerate others' difficult behaviour when you're stuck with them (e.g. a work colleague) or end a relationship when you believe that it's futile to spend any more time and energy trying to promote change in him or her.

Attempt to resolve a dispute rather than remain stuck with it

Passive-aggressiveness refers to a person expressing his anger indirectly through such actions as silence, sarcasm, sulking, withdrawing affection, or not following through on commitments or promises despite his initial assurances to the contrary. The purpose of these various actions is to hurt, frustrate or punish others, to get back at them in some way for what he perceives has been done to him. The person usually denies he is feeling angry or being difficult when confronted about his behaviour. As Nay (2004: 35) remarks: 'Passive-aggression is perhaps the most difficult face of anger to deal with because the other person withholds or obstructs what you want but denies anger. How can you resolve a problem the other [person] won't admit exists?'

Leonora had made up her mind that one of her employees, Lucy, was passive-aggressive and even called her that: 'That's what she is. I looked on the internet, there it was. As I was reading it, it described her perfectly. She seems pleasant on the surface, but when she says she'll do things there are always excuses why it wasn't done or the work is done poorly. She puts me behind with my own work. I feel like strangling her sometimes.' If Leonora had indeed studied passive-aggressiveness, then she would know that labelling Lucy in this way is likely to rebound upon her: 'She said I had the problem, I was paranoid and needed to get some professional help. The cheek of the woman. I was left fuming.' If you accuse somebody of being passive-aggressive, they are very unlikely to agree with you and confess their misdeeds.

As I mentioned in the introduction to this chapter, the starting point for dealing with difficult people is to focus on your own attitudes to them and how these attitudes can lead to self-disturbance about their behaviour. With Lenora, she was full of demanding 'should' statements such as 'She shouldn't behave like that', 'She should carry out all of her duties' and 'I shouldn't have to work with somebody like that' and viewed Lucy as the devious enemy she had to keep watching in order to detect her next 'slippery' manoeuvre. When Leonora thought about Lucy's behaviour in this way or talked to others about it, she invariably ended up making herself angry. Leonora did not want to be stuck with anger as her only response option to Lucy's behaviour, so it was essential for Leonora to accept that other people act in accordance with their viewpoint and values, not hers, and to stop demanding that they should not be acting in the way they are undoubtedly acting at any given moment.

This acceptance does not mean passivity or helplessness, but the start of your attempts at constructive engagement with the person. Leonora found the concept of acceptance difficult to digest as it smacked of weakness and surrender, but was she advocating hanging on to her anger as the solution to the problem and would she teach this to others if she was running a workshop on dealing with difficult people? She knew this wasn't the way to deal with Lucy, so we then moved on to the next important step to accept – that she would be doing most of the work in trying to sort things out. So Leonora arranged a meeting with Lucy:

- She apologized for calling Lucy passive-aggressive (she had to swallow hard to do this).
- She brought into the open in a non-confrontational way what she saw as the problem, namely, Lucy's inability either to complete tasks she'd been assigned or the completed tasks were done poorly, and invited her not only to comment on this but also to discuss any interpersonal difficulties that she found in working with her.
- She was open-minded to the possibility that Lucy had legitimate grievances against her – she complained that Leonora overloaded her with work, didn't give her any praise and made

the deadlines too tight – and said there was some truth in these points which she would address.

- She frequently summarized Lucy's viewpoint in an attempt to convince her that her concerns were being listened to.
- She presented a preview (Nay, 2004) of what behavioural changes she now expected from Lucy – tasks done competently and completed within the agreed time – and what would be the consequences of failing to do this: initially, some coaching in time and task management skills would be offered, but if there was no improvement disciplinary action would be taken.

With the air cleared, they did develop a more productive and professional relationship though some tension remained. Disciplinary action was not necessary. Looking back, Leonora thought it was strange that she viewed her anger as a sign of strength in the face of what she saw as Lucy's recalcitrant behaviour and to give it up meant that Lucy had won the power struggle: 'By doing that, I thought I would have allowed her to get away with her poor performance. In fact, what I thought was inner strength was actually inner stagnation as I really couldn't see any way of changing this situation. I was looking at her doing the changing, not me taking the situation in a very different direction.'

Learning to tolerate criticism by examining your reactions to it

Kevin loved his father, phoned him regularly and went to see him every weekend he could. His father was in his early seventies and lived alone, his wife having died a few years earlier. Kevin said he would go in a good mood to see his father but come home in a bad one. 'It's like a ritual. I go hoping that this weekend will be different but, no, he starts having a go at me again and I keep thinking, "What's the bloody point?" I drive home in a foul mood and my wife shakes her head and says, "You only bring it on yourself by continually going over there. When will you learn?"' So what was going on when Kevin went to visit his father?

KEVIN: He does a lot of moaning about things in general, which I don't mind, but when he gets personal that's when my hackles start to rise.

MICHAEL: Can you give me an example of him getting personal?

KEVIN: Yes. He says I let myself down by becoming a vet rather than training to be what he calls a 'proper doctor' like he was. That's one of his favourite criticisms. I've explained my reasons to him many times but he doesn't accept them.

MICHAEL: Do you know why you need to keep justifying to him why you became a vet instead of a 'proper doctor'?

KEVIN: I'm not sure. He has a go at my brother and sister for what he thinks they've done wrong with their lives but they take it in their stride. They always say, 'It's just Dad's way. He's not going to change now, is he?' It doesn't upset them like it does me. I wish I could be more like them.

MICHAEL: Imagine that the next time you visit him and he starts on you, you don't respond or justify your actions, what then?

KEVIN: I wish I could do that but I'd feel very uncomfortable doing that.

MICHAEL: Because . . .?

KEVIN: Because . . . [shaking his head in disbelief] I still need to get his approval for the important decisions I've made in my life. That's what I'm trying to do each time unsuccessfully.

MICHAEL: And if he withholds his approval for these important decisions?

KEVIN: Then I start to doubt myself. Maybe I should have trained as a GP like he did. Other things he picks on are: I should have sent my children to private schools rather than to state schools, I should have pushed them all harder to get to university and so on. These things raise doubts in my mind and I start arguing with myself on the way home. Is he right?

MICHAEL: So his criticisms and lack of approval for your important decisions feed into your existing doubts. You bring these doubts with you when you visit your father. Is that an accurate summary?

KEVIN: Yes, that's right. I didn't think of it like that. I thought he was responsible for deflating my good mood.

MICHAEL: He can't do that without considerable help from you. So if you want to take his criticisms in your stride like your brother and sister, what will you need to do?

KEVIN: Grow up! At my age, to stop seeking his approval for what I've done with my life and have the courage of my convictions for the life that I've actually led.

Kevin's injunction to himself to 'grow up' turned out to be unnecessary. The more we examined the situation, the more he realized that if he truly needed his father's approval for important life decisions then he would have chosen what his father wanted him to do – which he never did. For example, his father thought that his son was marrying the 'wrong sort of woman' but Kevin went ahead and married her anyway. What we eventually focused on was his anger with himself for continuing to have doubts about these decisions when, in retrospect, he said he still wouldn't have decided any differently. The doubts had become habitual and reinforced each time he went to see his father: 'I suppose I keep thinking these doubts contain some truths that I don't want to see.' Every time he engaged with the doubts, particularly when he attempted to justify his decisions to his father, he just strengthened them and thereby made them seem more credible.

He agreed to do some imagery exercises whereby the doubts were activated but he didn't engage with them, just noticed they were there and let them pass through his mind. Through repeated practice of this technique of non-engagement with the thoughts, known as mindfulness, they withered away. Now when Kevin went to see his father, he no longer felt the need to defend his decisions when they were criticized. He said that sometimes he would sit there quietly letting his father's criticisms wash over him. On other occasions, he would interrupt his father and suggest they go for a walk or look at the garden which turned the conversation in a different direction. Kevin's wife noticed that he now returned home in a good mood rather than the foul mood of old. Why did he keep having a go at Kevin? 'He was a loving father but always a critical one and it just got worse since his wife died. I still look forward to seeing him, but now I've learnt how not to upset myself when I'm with him.'

Standing up to a bullying boss

Bullying bosses don't pay any attention to the management maxim: 'Praise in public, criticise in private.' They are likely to tear you off a strip wherever you are, whenever they feel like it. You've been publicly humiliated and harbour fantasies of revenge. You complain to others about his behaviour and receive their commiserations – 'He's like that with everyone' – but complaining without formulating a constructive (not vengeful) action plan to stand up for yourself makes you feel even more helpless in the face of his outbursts and fearful of the next ones. How to deal with a bully then? The first step is to see your boss as a project you've assigned yourself to work on: to develop empathy (understand the world from his perspective, but you don't have to agree with it) for someone you can't stand and often hope will be hit by a two ton truck; but remember, your goal is not to feel sorry for him but to attempt to neutralize his bullying. So your detective work is a means towards that end.

Just as various household appliances come with a user manual in order for you to get the best out of them, see your boss as having a user manual and your job is to understand what makes him tick so you can get the best out of your contact with him. Insisting that his obnoxious behaviour should be different from what it actually is will not alter his behaviour as he is operating according to his own user manual, not the one you have in your mind for him such as 'Managers should treat their staff fairly, equally and respectfully' and 'Managers have a duty of care to their employees for their physical and psychological health'.

What usually motivates such bosses is their intense focus on getting the job done (Brinkman and Kirschner, 2002; Persaud, 2005) and you're seen as either helping or hindering their goal-directed efforts. While you probably see yourself as the innocent victim who has to endure your boss's frequent tongue-lashings, he might see himself as the real victim because your bungling and inefficiency are going to make him look bad in his own and/or others' eyes through underperformance – his bullying is often driven by his own insecurities. While you will no doubt take exception to being verbally abused, such managers often believe their attacks are 'nothing personal' (Brinkman and Kirschner, 2002), just their way of lighting a fire under you to get the results from you that they want. So 'reading' from your boss's user manual, you need to align yourself with his goals by being as task-focused as he is (Persaud, 2005). His concerns are yours too. However, when under verbal attack from him you may adopt the following stance:

1   Be calm but resolute in getting your points across. Don't engage in a slanging match with him, grovel before him or make lots of whimpering excuses. You will probably find it hard to interrupt him, so you might want to wait until he has exhausted himself and start with something like 'If you've now finished . . .' unless he storms off at the end of his harangue.

Even if you haven't had a chance to respond, your coolness under fire contrasts sharply with his temper tantrums. He's not used to this response from you. In my experience, such bosses start to feel embarrassed about their own behaviour when they see the calmness of yours.

2   Keep interrupting him by using his name if the harangue doesn't appear to be coming to an end (e.g. 'Mr Johnson. Could I stop you there?') until you have his attention (Dryden and Gordon, 1994). Keep your comments brief and to the point and in your best task-focused voice ask: 'What *precisely* is the problem with the work I've done?' If he starts lashing out again, interrupt and remind him that he isn't offering you any task-focused information in order for you to understand what you've done wrong and, more importantly, what you can do to put it right in order to support his goals; therefore, time is being wasted with his harangues. Make sure you're not attacking him but respectfully and forcefully directing his attention to putting matters right. If you believe that you haven't made mistakes, ask him for evidence – you're not interested in insults – to support his case.

3   Do your best to gain his respect. Hauck (1998: 39) suggests that a definition of respect is mild fear: 'If you want respect from people you must make them somewhat afraid of you.' Even though he is your boss and has the power to make your life at work difficult, it's important to show him that you're not intimidated by this fact or his outbursts. While remaining cool under fire, you can keep on emphasizing that you wish to be treated with respect, not contempt, and that you're no longer going to tolerate being spoken to in this way and will terminate the conversation as soon as the verbal fireworks start: 'Speaking to me like that adds nothing of value or clarity to problem solving and certainly does not motivate me to work harder on your behalf.' You will need to be consistent in applying this new assertive approach as wavering between firmness and fearfulness, calmness and cringing is likely to indicate to him that a few more verbal onslaughts will put you back in your place and end your rebellion as you haven't got the courage to see it through.

If you remain firm and calm, he's likely to look at you in a new way, as if he's really seeing you for the first time as a person rather than as an employee to be kicked around when he's angry. You're likely to win his grudging respect for standing your ground – the key indicator will be a significant decline in the frequency, intensity and duration of his broadsides (but don't expect them to disappear completely). As Brinkman and Kirschner (2002: 72) observe: 'Aggressive people actually like assertive people who stand up for themselves, as long as the assertiveness isn't perceived as an attack.' Let him have the last word in your discussions as your way of acknowledging he is the boss and if his last word is a dig at you, let it pass. You've learnt how to manage your manager which now makes your life at work much better than it was a few months before. Being treated with respect is an important element in your user manual which your boss has now inserted into his, if somewhat begrudgingly.

Removing guilt to give you more freedom of action

'Doesn't she ever stop moaning?' This may be a frequent complaint of yours about someone in your life yet you can end up moaning continually about the moaner as if this is the only response open to you. Additionally, you say her moaning drives you up the wall yet continue to listen to it while fuming inside – 'Why can't she stop moaning and talk about something pleasant for a change?' What you don't seem to realize is that you're helping to maintain such behaviour by giving her your attention, often for as long as she wants it, when you're desperate to get on with other things. Continual complainers can be seen as helping to drain the energy out of you, thereby leaving you feeling weak, exhausted and irritable. After all, you're fighting on two fronts: externally, trying to look interested when you're not, making expressions of sympathy while trying ineffectually to end the conversation and get away; and internally, raging at the person for boring you, constraining you, dumping on you, and at yourself for continually allowing yourself to be put in this position. But why do you let it occur? The usual answer is guilt. Sue's friend, Jo, seemed to fall into one crisis after another and wanted to tell Sue every twist and turn of each one. Sue was fed up with being the unwilling listener to Jo's endless troubles, but not fed up enough.

SUE: The other evening she phoned. I wanted an early night after an exhausting day at work, but she was upset, crying, she was in quite a state. She had another bust-up with her husband and I thought, 'Not tonight, not again, I'm so tired.'

MICHAEL: Did you tell her?

SUE: I wanted to but I didn't.

MICHAEL: Do you know what held you back from telling her?

SUE: If I said that to her, she'd be hurt. She'd probably get even more upset, think I didn't care. I'd feel bad.

MICHAEL: Do you know which emotion 'bad' refers to?

SUE: I'm not sure.

MICHAEL: Imagine that you have told her you want an early night and you'll talk to her tomorrow. So you're now going to bed knowing that she is still upset, crying.

SUE: You're making me feel guilty putting it like that.

MICHAEL: How would *you* feel if *you* did what *you* wanted to do – which was to go to bed early?

SUE: I would feel guilty.

MICHAEL: Without my assistance [client nods]. Do you know what you'd be thinking to make yourself feel guilty?

SUE: Well, I'm her friend and I'm letting her down when she needs my help. I'm not being a good friend. I've hurt her. I've made her feel even worse than she already is. It's like I've abandoned her. Even if I had gone to bed, I wouldn't be able to sleep because what I'd done would be playing on my mind. Can't win, can I? Stay and listen, feel resentful; don't listen and go to bed, feel guilty.

MICHAEL: How would you like to respond when Jo tells you about her troubles?

SUE: Sometimes to listen but not endlessly, and for me to learn how to bring it to an end rather than waiting for her to do it, and at other times tell her I'm not in the mood to listen because I've got my own things to get on with.

MICHAEL: And if she gets upset with your new approach . . .?

SUE: To somehow realize that it's not my fault she gets upset, without me feeling guilty about it. I can't be more specific than that.

MICHAEL: Okay. Let's start with the guilt.

In Table 2.1 (p. 30), the themes linked to guilt are moral lapse and hurting others. The thoughts of a person feeling guilty would reflect these themes. In the cognitive dynamics of guilt, you think you should have done something you didn't do (sin of omission) or you did something you shouldn't have done (sin of commission) and therefore have violated your moral code. Such bad behaviour means you're a bad person (which was what Sue was referring to when she said 'I feel bad'). In Sue's case, her moral code regarding friendship with Jo was 'I must always be there for her when she is in trouble and if I'm not, then I've let her down and am a bad person for not only doing this but also for causing her even more distress than she is already experiencing by letting her down.' Sue's moral code was expressed rigidly and harshly, thereby allowing her no room for psychological manoeuvre, i.e. she denied herself the option of sometimes not wanting to listen to Jo's troubles and even if she did choose that option, she could expect to feel the full force of her guilt beliefs. If Sue's beliefs drove her guilt, then Jo's beliefs drove her hurt feelings if Sue didn't want to listen such as: 'When I'm upset, Sue must be there for me. If she's not interested in listening, then she's let me down. I don't deserve to be treated like that when I'm already upset. She's not a friend to me. I'm all alone in my time of need.' (I know I'm speculating about Jo's beliefs but, in my experience, such beliefs are usually present when you're feeling hurt.)

As Sue was the author of her rigid moral code regarding her friendship with Jo, she decided to rewrite it in flexible and compassionate terms that gave her the room for manoeuvre which was previously lacking: 'I'll listen sometimes but not for long periods. She always asks for my advice but never pays any attention to it. It's not my job to sort out her problems. If she gets upset when I don't want to listen, then so be it. I'm not responsible for how she feels, she is! There's nothing bad about me for not wanting to listen, so it's ridiculous for me to condemn myself for turning a deaf ear. I wouldn't condemn others in a similar position to myself.' Sue wanted her new view to be concise rather than have to remember all of the above (a new viewpoint tends to be wordy as you're trying to see the problem in the round as opposed to the all or nothing rigidity of the old view), so she whittled it down to: 'To listen or not to listen – it depends on the circumstances.' With her new view in operation, Jo took umbrage when Sue chose sometimes not to listen to her latest tale of woe and the relationship eventually tailed off as Sue suspected it would.

What surprised Sue was why she put up with Jo's complaining for so long, 'It can't just be guilt, can it?' As Siebert (1999) asks, what benefits might you get from associating with someone who is

a continual moaner? Sue was initially perplexed by this question –
'There are no benefits' – but, on further reflection, she recalled that
after her gruelling sessions with Jo 'slagging off her husband', she
was able to reassure herself that at least her own marriage was
strong which reinforced her closeness to and love for her husband;
also, she felt better about herself generally: 'I have my faults like
anybody else but, thankfully, nothing like hers.' But, with hindsight, listening to Jo's moaning was too high a price to pay for such
reassurance which Sue could have got anyway by looking at the
evidence for it in her own life.

Learning not to disturb yourself about someone's hatred of you

In the section on dealing with a bullying boss (pp. 147–50), I
suggested some ways in which you could temper his aggressiveness
towards you, thereby improving the relationship you have with him
– still difficult but at least he displays a new-found respect for you.
With someone who hates you, you may not be able to make any
progress in influencing him to moderate his hateful attitudes
towards you. You don't have to do anything wrong or mean to be
hated: you can be hated just because of your ethnicity, gender,
sexuality, religion, class, lifestyle, success, looks, views, popularity
– the list goes on. Hermann Hesse, the German writer and poet,
observed, 'If you hate a person, you hate something in him that is
part of yourself. What isn't part of ourselves doesn't disturb us.'
For example, you may despise a work colleague for her grovelling
manner towards her boss which uncomfortably reminds you of
similar behaviour you previously engaged in and damned yourself
for; or you hate gays because you were sexually aroused when you
looked at a magazine full of naked men and were disgusted with
yourself for having such feelings which then called into question
your own vaunted full-blooded heterosexuality.

As always, your resilient response starts with self-management.
If there is a threat of physical violence you will need to defend
yourself if attacked or learn self-defence skills just in case. The
threat of physical aggression aside, don't fall into the trap of
interrogating yourself with such questions as 'What did I do to
make him hate me?' 'Make him' implies that his hatred of you is
involuntary, you did it to him, and he might actually like you if he
was able to choose for himself. You may dwell on your faults,

trying to find the roots of your 'badness' as a person to explain his hatred of you – he hasn't told you why he hates you so you're going to do the job for him. You have tried to speak to him on a number of occasions in an open-minded, conciliatory fashion, 'If you could just give me some idea of what I'm supposed to have done?', but he has snubbed you each time: 'Don't try that "I want to be your friend and let's all get along together" crap with me. Get lost!' You might want to ask yourself why you're working so hard to try to get him to change his view of you. Do you find it mentally distressing to live with the fact that someone hates you or that his hatred so brutally disrupts your view of yourself as a nice person? If he changed his mind about you, would your mental distress ease or your view of yourself become whole again? If this is the case, you've put the solution to these issues into the hands of the person who hates you!

You've tried to be reasonable with him but nothing works, so you decide to play him at his own game – hatred for hatred. But that would be a dangerous game to play: 'Hatred can consume you more than almost any other feeling and, like jealousy and a few other passions, can literally obsess you and run your life' (Ellis, 1977: 221). Instead of pursuing your own interests, more and more of your life is focused on him, thereby you start to lose your sense of self, or the only sense of self that you now recognize is an embittered one – 'He did this to me'. You may end up hating yourself for turning into this 'twisted person'. The irony of hatred is summed up by Olsen (quoted in Ellis, 1977: 221): 'Hate is a means by which we punish and destroy ourselves for the actions of others.'

For example, a client of mine who was involved in a car crash suffered continual pain as a result of her injuries (the driver, who had stolen the car which hit her, ran away from the scene and was never caught). She was very angry and developed an intense hatred towards him for 'ruining my life'. She saw her anger as a form of retribution that would one day 'catch up with him' – she didn't know when or how this would happen – and then he would suffer like she did. To give it up would mean that 'he's got away with it, he's won'. The corrosive physical and psychological effects of her prolonged anger took a heavy toll on her life including exacerbating the pain she suffered. The anger and hatred were the self-destroying elements, not the injuries themselves. Unfortunately, I didn't make any headway in trying to help her see and change what she was doing to herself.

So, how do you respond when someone hates you and it appears he's not going to change his mind no matter what you do? The first step is to accept, however reluctantly, the reality of the situation by reminding yourself that you're not immune from being hated (e.g. 'I would strongly prefer not to be hated but there is no reason why it must not happen to me'). Try to adopt a stance of indifference towards his hatred of you as intended by the Stoic philosophers (see Epictetus in Chapter 2, p. 21): to distinguish between what we can and cannot control: 'We should be concerned about the things we can control, and not about the things we can't control. This is a central piece of Stoic advice that has reverberated down through the ages' (Morris, 2004: 86). If you're not keen on this idea of cultivating indifference to being hated, you can choose to adopt the statement based on preferences in the above example.

When I was at college several decades ago, one of my classmates hated me for reasons she didn't properly explain apart from saying I was 'horrible and unpleasant'. I was quite troubled by her hatred of me – she gave me 'filthy looks' every time I passed her in the corridor which I added to my worries – and I did my best to try and be pleasant to her, but to no avail. I racked my brains trying to work out what I had done to offend her but couldn't put my finger on it. The course would last for another 18 uncomfortable months it seemed. However, one morning on the train to college I suddenly decided (actually the result of much reflection) that if she hates me, so be it – and I felt relieved, a relief which endured. I had secured an inner freedom from her hatred of me. I didn't need her to give up her hatred in order to set me free. Now when I passed her in the corridor I smiled the smile of freedom and when I sat near her in the classroom I felt relaxed instead of worrying about what dark thoughts she might be having about me.

You can't change his hatred towards you, but you can control whether you disturb yourself about it. If you do disturb yourself about his hatred of you, you will be trapped in a form of psychological servitude. This means that your disturbance is likely to continue for as long as his hatred of you does because you won't let go of the ideas that you've done nothing wrong to be hated and it's unfair, and it's an intolerable situation to have to endure. Additionally, you base your actions on how he might view them – 'I don't want to give him more ammunition to fire at me' – thereby making yourself a prisoner within his mind, so to speak. You look at yourself through his view of you and act in ways that you hope will lessen his hatred towards you, or at least not make it worse.

When you come into unavoidable contact with the person who hates you (maybe at work or in social settings), keep the conversation brief and formal. Don't 'bite' if they start to make nasty comments. Terminate the conversation and walk away. Don't worry about him seeing it as a sign of weakness; if you do worry about this, you will be putting yourself back into psychological servitude. Through your actions, you're letting him know what is and isn't acceptable behaviour, severely circumscribing his room for malicious manoeuvre in your presence.

However, it will be harder to curtail what he does behind your back like spreading unsavoury rumours about you which you will need to treat like background noise that you refuse to tune into; or if these rumours are causing some damage to your reputation and you want to deal with him face to face, make sure someone else is there who is impartial and in authority to mediate the discussion if it happens in the workplace. In some situations, you won't be able to walk away, such as in a meeting. If this is the case, then let him know in a firm tone of voice that you will not respond to insults, only to comments or questions that are phrased in a professional manner and give him an example to follow. There may be no easy answers to dealing with this kind of problem when you see the person on a regular basis. Demanding that there should be will only add to your difficulties.

Keep a sense of perspective about him: he's a minor irritant in your life when set against the goals you're working towards and the enjoyment you get from family and friends. If you agree with the notion that no experience has to be wasted as there is always learning to be extracted from it, then having an enemy can help you to define more clearly what qualities are important to you – such as reason, tolerance, equality, cooperation and civility – by what you don't want for yourself: that hatred could ever supplant reason as the guiding force for your attitudes and actions in life (you presumably would want to teach this to your children too). To sum up this section, learn to carry lightly in your mind his hatred of you.

Allow others to find their own way in life

Annie would tear her hair out over what she described as her 23-year-old daughter's lack of 'get up and go': 'She just drifts through life. She didn't push herself at school. She's in and out of jobs, can't seem to hold one down. More interested in going to rock concerts than finding a career for herself. Boyfriends come and go. Flat's a mess. Doesn't care about getting into debt. Every time I speak to her about these issues she just shrugs her shoulders. She makes me so mad with her attitude to everything.' Annie sent herself into overdrive on her daughter's behalf but didn't get back the changes she was hoping to see in her. She often paid off her daughter's debts and cleaned her flat hoping to motivate her into doing these things for herself. 'When she comes round for Sunday dinner I keep hoping she's going to say she's seen the error of her ways, but she hardly speaks and then can't wait to leave once she's finished her dinner.' Trying to force her daughter out of her 'lethargic state', as Annie called it, wasn't working and was accelerating the deterioration of their relationship, so why was Annie persisting with an unproductive strategy?

ANNIE: She's my daughter. I want to see her fulfil her potential, to get the best out of life. But she's not doing that. She's going downhill. I can't be happy while my daughter is in this state.

MICHAEL: What does your daughter say about all this?

ANNIE: Well, she would say, 'Just leave me alone, stop interfering and let me do things my own way.' But if I leave her alone she'll get worse.

MICHAEL: What does your husband say?

ANNIE: 'She's made her own bed, so she'll have to lie in it.' He isn't any help. I sometimes think she takes after him. It's always the same: mothers fight to the bitter end for their children while the fathers give up and hide behind their newspapers or retreat to the pub.

MICHAEL: Do you have a 'bitter end' in mind for your daughter?

ANNIE: That she's going to waste her life, make nothing of it.

MICHAEL: Can you predict so accurately the course of her life?

ANNIE: I think so. That's why I'm fighting so hard.

MICHAEL: What would it cost you to step back and not interfere in her life as she wants you to do?

ANNIE: It would cost me a great deal: stand idly by while her life falls apart. You're not serious, are you?

MICHAEL: Well, she doesn't pay any attention to your advice, does she? You're not making any positive impact on her decision-making. Your relationship with her is nearing the point of no return if you're not careful. She says let her do things her own way, so why can't you let her?

ANNIE: Because if I keep an eye on her, then I'll be there to stop things getting worse.

MICHAEL: You said earlier that she's going downhill, from your point of view, even though you're keeping an eye on her. Why don't you give her the benefit of the doubt and let her get on with her own life: debts, messy flat, rock concerts, succession of boyfriends and jobs, and all?

ANNIE: Just give up on her?

MICHAEL: I'm not suggesting that. You're not going to abandon her. You'd step in if things got truly worse, but stop the interfering. Do you want her to lead an independent life – her way, not your way?

ANNIE: Of course I do. She's my daughter. I love her.

MICHAEL: If you mean it, then try a different approach. Allow her to live her life, mistakes and all.

ANNIE: [sighs] You mean stand back.

MICHAEL: Yes, stand back.

ANNIE: [wearily] Okay. I'll give it a try. I'm exhausted through worrying about her.

Standing back meant no uninvited visits to her daughter's flat, no cleaning it or paying off her debts, no prying into her affairs unless her daughter brought them up. Needless to say, Annie felt a tremendous pull to do the opposite of what she had agreed to do (she resisted this urge most of the time) and imagined her daughter's life spiralling downwards into squalor and hopelessness (which didn't happen). When her daughter came round for Sunday dinner, she asked her mother to pay off her current debts – this was one piece of maternal meddling that she didn't object to – and Annie reluctantly refused: 'You said you didn't want me to interfere in your life and I'm not going to. They're your debts and you'll have to sort them out from now on.' Her daughter stormed off and didn't speak to her for several weeks. Annie fretted during this period, wondering if she was doing the right thing. She realized that the primary struggle was with herself, not with her daughter: 'I was the most difficult person in this situation. I was coming round to my husband's point of view which was bringing us closer again. I thought he didn't care about her, but he cared in his own way. I found out something I didn't like about myself, that I sounded like a tyrant – my daughter had to live her life my way and my husband had to see things my way.'

I asked Annie to list her daughter's strengths in contrast to her usual focus on what she perceived as her weaknesses. She was perplexed. 'What strengths?' I suggested that her daughter was able to live alone, she found the flat herself, she could get jobs and attract boyfriends, and enjoyed life with her friends including going to rock concerts. If her daughter never had a job, stayed in her flat all the time and was depressed, dependent on drink and drugs, then Annie would really have something to worry about. Initially she wanted to rebut all the strengths I'd mentioned and turn them into faults, but in trying to see the world through her daughter's eyes she reluctantly agreed, then started crying: 'Why am I so negative about my daughter? This has got to stop.'

So she arranged to take her daughter out for a meal and opened her heart to her, including telling her that she was in therapy, what she had been learning about herself and what changes she'd been making. There was a reconciliation of sorts. Her daughter was still somewhat suspicious as to whether her mother would keep her word not to interfere in her life while Annie stuck to her guns in refusing to pay off her debts. Her daughter held down a job for much longer than usual to pay them off and, Annie said, was now much more careful about incurring them since 'mother's safety net' had been removed. Annie pointed to the Sunday dinner with her daughter as a mark of real progress: 'She stays for an hour or two after lunch and we chat about this and that, even have some laughs. I haven't felt relaxed in my daughter's company in a long time.' As with the discussion in the previous section about freeing yourself from psychological servitude, Annie no longer tied her happiness to her daughter leading the kind of life that she had envisaged for her.

Dealing with difficult people starts with self-management

When you deal with people you perceive to be difficult, don't fall into the psychological trap of demanding that they should be acting other than they are as this is like insisting that day should be night and vice versa. You're likely to make yourself upset that your demands are falling on deaf ears. Remember, other people's actions flow from their viewpoint, not yours. If you accept their behaviour (but not approve of it), then you've avoided adding self-disturbance to your problem-solving efforts. It's up to you to find out what makes them tick – see the world from their frame of reference – and what steps might be needed in order to influence their behaviour positively. You only have the ability to influence their behaviour, changing it is up to them. So don't berate yourself for being unable to change it (self-disturbance slipping in again). You're not omnipotent! On other occasions, the best course of action to take with a difficult person is not to attempt to influence his behaviour, but to detach yourself from him as the relationship has outlived its usefulness for you and is now a drain on your time and energy. Sometimes the most difficult person you have to deal with is yourself and it takes personal courage to admit this.

Responding resiliently to whatever is thrown at you in life is a great set of skills to have and, like all skills, requires constant practice to maintain and improve them. This is the focus of the next chapter.

Chapter 9

Maintaining resilience

Introduction

In this book I have looked at developing resilience from a cognitive behavioural perspective – pinpointing which attitudes and behaviours are likely to help or hinder you in facing adversity – and presented many case examples of individuals struggling successfully (most of the time) against the odds. Overcoming these adverse events usually changes the way you see yourself: for example, from diffident to determined about exerting greater control over the direction of your life. However, there is no guarantee that your resilience skills are now fixed in perpetuity and will automatically be in evidence when you face the next challenge in your life. One of the most important lessons from therapy is the need to maintain your gains (what you've learnt) on a lifelong basis. Formal therapy is over but the rest of your life stretches out before you, so how are you going to manage this new learning? As an analogy, think about the difference between getting fit (going from near collapse at the start of training to being able to run a half-marathon at the end of training) and staying fit (being able to run half-marathons on a regular basis to prevent a decline in your performance).

Some clients believe, despite my warnings to the contrary, that their hard-won changes will stay in place independently of whatever they may do (e.g. occasional 'treats' of cocaine won't interfere with your abstinence approach to drug use or continuing to lose your temper on a frequent basis is acceptable because you've learnt anger management skills to bring yourself under control again). With this self-deluding attitude towards maintaining change, you're likely to encourage, if not invite, a setback to occur, and if more setbacks follow you'll probably slide all the way back to the point at which you first attended therapy. Your self-defeating beliefs, behaviours and feelings are resurgent and it seems that all your gains from therapy have been wiped out. Therefore, complacency about maintaining your changes is really self-sabotage.

What is required from you is hard work and determination to maintain them – a commitment to safeguard your resilience skills from decaying through infrequent use or disuse. This commitment won't protect you from setbacks, no matter how much you want to avoid them, as they are part of the post-therapy progress of fallible (imperfect) human beings. But your approach to dealing with them is the key factor, namely, not to upset yourself unduly about them and to focus on what learning can be extracted from these setbacks in order to correct your behaviour (see Dealing with setbacks, pp. 168–73). As I've said on a number of occasions in this book, no experience, whatever it is, has to be wasted if you're prepared to examine it for productive lessons to be learnt. So what steps can you take you maintain your resilient outlook?

Remember your ABCs

In Chapter 2, I introduced the ABC model of thinking. This model shows the powerful influence that our beliefs have on how we feel and act towards events:

A = adversity
B = beliefs about adversity
C = consequences – emotional and behavioural

To recap, within the model there are two forms of thinking: A→C thinking, i.e. events or others make us feel and act in the way that we do (e.g. 'My wife leaving me made feel worthless and started me drinking. I can't be happy without her. Time will never heal me. I'll never get over it'); and B→C thinking, i.e. how our beliefs, rather than events or others, powerfully affect how we feel and act (e.g. 'I miss my wife but my self-worth remains intact. I'm not going to seek solace in alcohol. It's difficult presently to feel happy without her but I know happiness will return. Time doesn't necessarily heal; it's what I do with the time that counts'). A→C thinking is likely to keep you feeling trapped, acting like a victim, helpless to direct your own destiny whereas B→C thinking encourages you to take personal responsibility for how you think, feel and act thereby making you the author of your life experiences. Record ABC examples in your learning diary (see pp. 167–8) to determine how well or badly you are coping with current difficulties: 'Am I thinking A→C or B→C in this situation?'

Even though there is always more than one way of looking at a situation, it may not always be immediately apparent what this alternative viewpoint might be. A structured way of stimulating your thinking is to ask yourself the questions which I discussed in Chapter 2 and elsewhere in this book. If you believe, for example, 'I can't stand having to persist with things I don't enjoy doing', ask yourself whether this belief is:

(a) *Rigid or flexible?* 'Rigid. It doesn't allow me to see that there are other ways of responding to doing unenjoyable tasks, so every year, for example, I get myself into a right old state over doing my tax return. I've put myself in a mental straitjacket.'

(b) *Realistic or unrealistic?* 'Unrealistic. If I really couldn't stand persisting with unenjoyable tasks, then I wouldn't be able to complete any of them. However, I do throw in the towel on a lot of occasions, not because I genuinely can't stand persisting with them, but because I treat this belief as true and, on that basis, give up.'

(c) *Helpful or unhelpful?* 'Unhelpful. I get angry about having to do such tasks. This makes them seem unbearable to carry on with and I'm more likely to give up at that point which, of course, makes it even less likely that I'll want to get on with the next dull task that comes along. Also, I'm not a nice person to be around when I'm in this mood. I get into an adult version of the terrible twos that children have.'

(d) *Would you teach it to others?* 'No. There are many things in life that we don't like doing but it's in our interests to do them such as getting my tax return in on time to avoid incurring a fine; if we avoided persisting with them, imagine the unpleasant consequences for our lives. I certainly don't teach this belief to my children. I want them to grow up mentally strong, not shrinking away from difficult things.'

So what might be an alternative belief that emerges from this structured examination? For example, 'I don't like doing unenjoyable tasks, but I can stand persisting with them as it's in my interests to do so.' This new belief can be subjected to the same examination as your 'I can't stand having to persist with things I don't enjoy doing' belief. Is your alternative belief:

(a) *Rigid or flexible*? 'Flexible. It allows me to state my dislike of doing dull tasks yet encourages me to persist in doing them.'
(b) *Realistic or unrealistic*? 'Realistic. I can stand persisting with them because I'm doing so. That's the evidence of my own eyes. I'm completing more tasks now than I did before, but I still give up at times because I'm listening again to the old belief.'
(c) *Helpful or unhelpful*? 'Helpful. That horrible anger is largely gone though I still feel somewhat irritated at times. I know I don't have to be happy about doing them. My wife says I'm more approachable now. When the next boring task comes along, I sigh deeply but nevertheless get stuck into it. I'm working my way through the tasks I've been avoiding or gave up on.'
(d) *Would you teach it to others*? 'Definitely. Increasing your level of frustration tolerance helps you to lead a more disciplined life. You learn that what you believe you can't stand you actually can, you get more done and feel more in control of your life which I'm sure most people would want to feel.'

Sometimes this structured approach to belief examination does not yield a satisfactory alternative viewpoint and more reflection is required before something more persuasive emerges. So be patient. Going for walks for a 'deep think', listening to music, reading resilience literature or talking to friends might deliver something better. Sometimes you may decide to have a rest from thinking about the issue because you appear to be trapped in a cognitive cul-de-sac and are then surprised when a new way of looking at the situation pops into your mind ('Where did that come from? I wasn't thinking about it'). You have, in fact, still been working on it but outside of your conscious awareness. As Myers (2004: 15) notes:

> You process vast amounts of information off screen. You effortlessly delegate most of your thinking and decision making to the masses of cognitive workers busily at work in your mind's basement. Only the really important mental tasks reach the executive desk, where your conscious mind works. When you are asked, 'What are you thinking?' your mental

CEO [chief executive officer] answers, speaking of worries, hopes, plans, and questions, mindless of all the lower-floor laborers.

Problem-solving is carried on at both conscious and non-conscious levels. So you're working on your problem even when you don't realize you are as those 'masses of cognitive workers' are still beavering away figuring out new possibilities for you.

Regular psychological workouts

Set yourself regular challenges in order to keep yourself psychologically sharp. Remember, developing resilience is not an end point – 'After what I've been through, I know all about resilience' – and then you can rest on your laurels. For example, if you've worked hard to overcome your need for approval from others and believe that you have internalized self-acceptance, then continue to demonstrate that this is truly the case by putting yourself into situations where you might be criticized, ridiculed or rejected. Some examples:

- Putting forward your views when others might take great exception to being contradicted by you (I wouldn't advise it if you ran the risk of being physically hurt or jeopardizing your job prospects in some way – prudence should be the guide in these situations).
- Revealing things about yourself to others (I'm not suggesting you bare your soul to everyone) which might shock them, such as talking about a period of clinical depression you experienced or stating that you haven't had sex for ten years.
- Telling a friend who is consistently negative about other people that it's tiring and tedious having to listen to all this and stating what you would like to focus on instead.
- Praising your boss for doing a fine job when you will be condemned as a sycophant by some of your colleagues.
- Interrupting verbose work colleagues and asking them to get to the point as you have a busy schedule to keep to.

These examples are not meant to suggest that you have to prove to yourself every five minutes how self-accepting you are (if you do have to prove it continually, this might indicate how much you don't believe it), or be tiresomely provocative, but to indicate the need to monitor your approval-seeking tendencies which slip back into your thinking from time to time and thereby act as a reminder of what further work needs to be done: 'I don't need to be patted on the head by others and told what a nice person I am in order to justify my existence or continually please others to my own detriment.'

Another reason for regular psychological workouts is that you can slip into self-deception regarding your progress, i.e. you believe you're maintaining it when, in fact, it's being undermined by your actions. For example, you've struggled long and hard to get your finances in order and pull yourself out of debt. You believe you now have a 'No more debt!' outlook. However, you're slowly building up debt again but justifying it by reassuring yourself that 'it's not the kind of big debt I used to have, there's debt and then there's debt, isn't there?' But what you're doing now is the same process that got you into the previous financial mess. Each time you spend what you don't have you see it as a one-off event instead of standing back and looking at the cumulative effect of these one-off events. Eventually, the time may come when you ask yourself, 'How in heaven's name did this happen to me again?' In order to avoid this outcome, carry out a monthly review, for example, of your finances to see where the debt is building and, most importantly, practise some self-denial – just because you want it, you don't have to buy it – to get your finances back into the black.

Regular psychological workouts don't have to focus exclusively on your problem areas: challenges can be exhilarating ones such as parachuting or white water rafting or expressing your social responsibility through undertaking, for example, voluntary work at home and/or abroad. Psychological workouts provide opportunities for further personal growth.

Look for stories of resilience

Look in the media for stories of how people overcame adversity. As Grotberg (1999: 187) observes: 'Once you make resilience a goal in your life, you will be surprised at the number of examples of resilience you will find in your newspaper, [on television] or in the magazines you read.' Put the word 'resilience' into your computer search engine and explore the various websites that are identified. You can also read about the lives of highly resilient people. A popular read is Nelson Mandela's autobiography, *Long Walk to*

Freedom (1995), which details, among other events, his 27 years of imprisonment and his eventual triumphant emergence from prison, unbroken and unembittered by his experiences. Another book, which I discussed in Chapter 2, is Viktor Frankl's *Man's Searching for Meaning* (1985), his account of his life in the Nazi concentration camps and how meaning can be found even in the most barbarous circumstances.

If friends, relatives or colleagues have gone through and been strengthened by how they handled tough times and are willing to talk to you about them, then their stories can be sifted for valuable information to put into your resilience file. Of course, the obverse will also provide useful information – how some individuals didn't cope well with misfortune, but it's important to be tactful and empathic in your discussions with these individuals and not see them as 'failures' whose only role is to provide you with cautionary tales of what not to do when adversity strikes.

Keep a learning diary

To help process your experiences in a structured way, you can use the framework shown in Figure 9.1 or adapt it to your own requirements.

You can also put in your learning diary what went or is going well for you and why. For example: 'I stopped smoking six months ago and the urge to smoke is still pretty powerful. When I'm tempted, I withhold permission to indulge, tolerate the urge until it passes by getting on with other things. I keep in the forefront of my mind every day my longer term goal of staying stopped forever and thereby prevent myself from being overwhelmed by my desires at that moment or looking no further than the time it takes to smoke a cigarette, which was so often my behaviour in the past.'

More generally, your diary can include anything that you find helpful or instructive (e.g. 'I started giving to a charity, on a monthly basis, some money to help people in Africa have operations to cure their blindness. I can get so caught up sometimes in the insularity of my own life and struggles that I forget that many people are much worse off than me and their adversities dwarf the ones I experience. But these comparisons, which I hear many people make, are forgotten in five minutes. I don't want to forget and it helps me to keep a sense of perspective when I run into trouble.').

What was the situation?	Being stuck in a traffic jam for two hours.
How did I respond?	I was angry. It shouldn't have happened to me after a long day at the office. I began brooding on other things that I think are unfair in my life.
How would I have liked to respond?	To accept the reality of the situation and use the time productively such as listening to a discussion on the radio or just being able to sit quietly with myself without brooding on events, past or present.
What can I learn from this situation?	That I still have a strong tendency to feel sorry for myself when things don't turn out in my favour. This means I give myself a double dose of discomfort: the unpleasant situation itself and my angry brooding about it.
What will I do with this learning?	I will go over in my mind on a daily basis that I'm not immune from experiencing unfairness in life. When it happens, it's just unfortunate, nothing stronger than that.
Is it working?	It is. The other day a report I'd worked so hard on was criticized by my boss. I immediately felt incensed by his comments, but then checked myself by reminding myself forcefully that I should, not shouldn't, experience what I see as unfairness from time to time. The world doesn't run to my convenience or revolve around my values. Then I got on with sorting out the report.

Figure 9.1 Learning diary

Dealing with setbacks and relapses

As I discussed in Chapter 1, expecting that you will be resilient at all times, under all circumstances – a perfectly maintained resilience – is a myth. Experiencing setbacks is part of the change process as well as the behaviour of fallible human beings. If you believe your progress should be uninterrupted, where did you get this idea from (it's an idea that will weaken your resilient outlook)? No matter how often I discuss with my clients the probability of post-therapy setback(s), some will cling to the idea that it won't happen to them, and so hits them much harder when it does.

A resilient approach to dealing with a setback is to accept its occurrence and tackle it as promptly as possible. Don't ignore it. A key question to ask yourself is: 'What attitudes brought about this setback?' These attitudes are likely to be a reactivation of the ones you've been attempting to change. For example, you're avoiding a speaking engagement because you're worrying again about doing a less than 'perfect job' and thereby making your self-worth conditional on the outcome. In this context, challenge this attitude by going over again that you're seeking to internalize self-acceptance – decoupling yourself from your behaviour – but preventing yourself from deepening your conviction in this idea by avoiding the speaking engagement. You want to do the best job you can, but it doesn't have to be perfect. Once you get this clear in your mind, then go ahead and speak. Whatever the outcome, reflect upon it in your learning diary.

Another worry about a setback is that it's the start of a slippery slope which you can't get off and your progress will be wrecked by the time you get to the bottom. As Warburton (2007: 132) points out:

> Typically, slippery slope arguments obscure the fact that in most cases we can decide how far down a slope we want to go: we can dig in our heels at a certain point and say 'here and no further' . . . The metaphor of slipperiness with its connotations of inevitable descent and frightening loss of control does not seem to allow this possibility. It conjures up images of powerlessness which may be inappropriate to the case in question.

In the above example, you might start avoiding all public speaking engagements and some social activities too where you believe your self-worth is on the line. You see your room for manoeuvre slowly shrinking to the point where only a few situations are deemed 'safe' for you to enter. However, the earlier you dig your heels in and say 'here and no further', the quicker you're likely to be in overcoming the setback(s). Therefore, from the top to the bottom of the slope there are a number of decision points along the way. This means, in essence, whether you give yourself permission to continue with your self-defeating behaviour or withhold permission in order to stop it. Continuing to give yourself permission is likely to result in a relapse, which is a full restoration of the problems you had when you first entered therapy.

If you do have a relapse, don't despair. Even though coming back from a relapse will probably be longer and harder than if you had a setback and you will need to reach deeper into yourself to reactivate your resilience strengths, such setbacks and relapses are instructive. They show you where you're still vulnerable (e.g. drinking excessively when under pressure at work or angrily refusing to accept that you're wrong when it's clearly evident that you are). These vulnerabilities demonstrate what additional skills you might need to learn such as acquiring some humility to admit you're wrong and/or that you're not practising enough the skills you already have, for example, the importance of consistently and forcefully challenging your resilience-undermining attitudes.

Hugh was a high achiever but he'd pushed himself too hard for too long which resulted in him taking extended sick leave as he was physically and psychologically spent. His lengthy recovery emphasized everything in moderation. His return to work was done on a gradual basis and for about two years he maintained a healthy balance between home and work. However, his old behaviour began to return and he ignored all the warning signs that he was slipping back. Eventually, he went off sick again (but for a shorter period), which was when I came into the picture.

HUGH: I can't understand how I could have been so stupid. I'd been doing so well. I could see the warning signs flashing. Why didn't I pay attention? All my progress has been wiped out.

MICHAEL: Well, the progress you made over the last two years remains intact, that can't be wiped out. You were doing the right things for a period of time which has now come to a temporary halt.

HUGH: How can you call it a 'temporary halt'? It feels like a disaster.

MICHAEL: Feelings aren't necessarily facts. I'm putting what you call a 'disaster' into the context of what you've achieved over the past two years. The most productive approach to dealing with a relapse is to see what we can learn from it rather than dwelling on what appears to you to be a disaster.

HUGH: What am I supposed to learn then?

MICHAEL: You said you didn't pay attention to the warning signs. Do you know why?

HUGH: I'm not sure.

MICHAEL: [tapping forehead] Think about giving yourself permission to override the warning signs.

HUGH: When I started pushing myself harder, I thought I was bound to feel some strain but that was understandable, so keep going.

MICHAEL: And as the strain got worse?

HUGH: I thought I'd be able to cope with it, so keep going.

MICHAEL: Did there come a point when you realized that you weren't coping with it?

HUGH: Yes, but I didn't pay attention. I didn't want to feel that same sense of defeat again when I was off ill the first time, so I battened down the hatches and hoped I would prevail, but I fell apart again. How damn stupid can a person be?

MICHAEL: It's important to continue to focus on the learning from this review of your relapse. Calling yourself stupid will distract you from doing that. Okay?

HUGH: Okay. Where were we?

MICHAEL: Falling apart again. Do you know what beliefs drove your high performance?

HUGH: I had to prove I was as good as my colleagues, if not better, and to do that I had to work much harder than them.

MICHAEL: And if you couldn't prove that, what would that mean about you?

HUGH: That I wasn't good enough, a fraud. I've had this belief for a long time and the only way to prevent being exposed as a fraud is to work much harder than anyone else. I keep feeling that I'm getting away with it, pulling the wool over people's eyes. I thought in those two years when I was working sensible hours, at a moderate pace, that those beliefs had disappeared, but then they came back with tremendous force and I went down in flames.

MICHAEL: Do you know if a specific event or incident triggered the re-emergence of those beliefs?

HUGH: A new manager came on board and he made some negative comments about me and I thought, 'I haven't pulled the wool over his eyes', so I got scared and went into overdrive to try and change his opinion of me.

MICHAEL: But you haven't changed your opinion of you.

HUGH: No. That's where I'm stuck. All roads lead back there.

MICHAEL: How would you like to see yourself?

HUGH: I know at one level I'm very competent with my work; if only I could really believe it, deep down.

MICHAEL: And if you were able to believe it deep down?

HUGH: All that worry I carry with me about being found out would be gone. I would feel so free, the burden has been lifted. I could relax more at work instead of keep having to prove myself all the time.

MICHAEL: Have you discussed this 'I'm really a fraud' belief with anyone before?

HUGH: I discussed it with the company doctor and I had a few sessions with a psychologist when I was ill the first time. I thought I'd sorted it out, but obviously not.

MICHAEL: Now's the time to bring that belief centre stage and give it a very detailed examination.

HUGH: It's long overdue. I'm determined this time to sort it out once and for all and stop seeing it as the real truth about me.

In essence, the examination focused on the following issues:

1   If he was really a fraud, then his company would have got rid of him a long time ago – he wasn't pulling the wool over anybody's eyes, his colleagues and managers were not fools.

2   He was put on the fast track to promotion graduate programme because of his potential but he didn't have a degree, so he considered himself intellectually inferior to his colleagues. In fact, he had demonstrated his intelligence and abilities in many ways and had risen faster than most on the programme.

3   If there were any criticisms of his work he immediately jumped to the conclusion that he'd been found out rather than seeing criticism as inevitable (no one is immune from it), and without there having to be any deeper significance to it.

4   He called himself a 'humble East End lad' who often thought he didn't deserve the success that he'd achieved. The word 'humble' reinforced his low estimation of himself as well as his incredulity at what he had achieved: 'The word is protective: if I am exposed as not good enough, I can defend myself by saying, "Well, what did you expect from a humble East End lad without a degree?"'

5   His exceptionally high standards had to be met on every occasion and if he fell below them this automatically meant he was a fraud, so he was continually judging himself by this 'falling short' criterion.

6   It was as if there were two DVDs to view about Hugh's life: one focused on the solid and substantial achievements he had

made at work (the reality) while the other showed him 'getting away with it, pulling the wool over people's eyes' (the fantasy). It was the second DVD through which he mainly processed his experiences at work.

This examination of his beliefs led him to shift his attention to processing his work experiences through the first DVD, not the second: Hugh the competent, not Hugh the fraud. Over time, he was able to gain the deeper conviction he was seeking that his abilities and achievements were based on genuine talent, not fraudulently contrived: 'Looking back, it's sad that I couldn't really believe in myself for all those years, but I finally got there. I now get more pleasure out of my work than I've ever done.' He kept a list of the warning signs of relapse in his office and was to take prompt corrective action if he noticed himself slipping back. At the end of our sessions he had regained a healthy work–life balance. That was several years ago, but we still have twice yearly booster sessions to monitor his progress. At the time of writing (December 2008), he's still maintaining his gains and Hugh the fraud is a distant memory, but Hugh the competent is still on the lookout for his reappearance, particularly when there is a lot of pressure at work.

When a setback isn't a setback

When your resilience skills appear to fail, it's easy to assume that you've fallen back in your progress. However, you might be encountering a situation you've never experienced before, like being stalked by a former boyfriend. So it's not a setback, just you entering unfamiliar territory. While you might not know at the present time what to do specifically about addressing this situation, your resilient outlook will guide your search for solutions: 'There is a way of dealing with this issue and I'm determined to find out what it is. I'm certainly not going to see myself as a helpless victim who puts her life on hold because of his behaviour.'

Talking about resilience

Teaching or talking to others about resilience is a good way of deepening your understanding of it. I don't mean by this that you advertise yourself as a paragon of resilience (the danger with this stance is becoming a 'resilience bore' and people turning the other way when they see you coming). If people are interested, you can discuss what you've learnt about being resilient and how it's a capacity open to all to learn. Some of my clients have told me, to their delight, that they have been able to teach their loved ones some resilience skills so they can benefit too. If you do teach resilience to others, be careful that in your own life there is not a divide between what you say and what you do. If there is, others will be quick to point out your hypocrisy and are likely to dismiss your views.

Look for role models

Don't be afraid to ask people how they cope with their difficulties and setbacks and still manage to achieve their goals (but don't act as an interrogator attempting to extract every last ounce of useful information from them). They can act as resilience role models. For example, you might admire someone at work who consistently meets all of her deadlines, a salesman who never gets demoralized over hearing the word 'no' when he makes a sales pitch or a relative who doesn't stay down for long whatever life throws at her. In my experience, people are usually only too willing to give you their philosophy of life. So don't stand on good manners, seek out this valuable information.

Strengthening your resilience through community involvement

'A host of studies has found that people who are involved with church or other religious communities have higher levels of resilience against life's knocks' (*The Times*, 11 October 2008). As well as the spiritual sustenance people get from their religious beliefs, Edelman (2006) points out that people with strong religious beliefs usually have good social support through what she calls 'communal fellowship'. Knowing that you're an integral part of this wider community may help you to cope better at times of crisis in your life in the sense that your struggle is shared and supported by others. A colleague told me that 'being part of my church gives me a deep sense of community. When I'm in trouble I know they will be supporting me in their thoughts and prayers which is very uplifting'. Pushing away others in order to lead a self-contained life may give the impression of self-control and mastery of one's destiny but can make your struggles harder to deal with if you keep insisting on fighting alone. The pastor Gordon MacDonald (2004: 217) states that 'living resiliently cannot be done alone'.

I'm not suggesting that you rush out and join your local church, but to consider the benefits of community involvement which widens the support that you can call on in time of need, which in turn can strengthen your own resolve (e.g. joining Alcoholics Anonymous to tackle alcohol dependence). Help is reciprocal: you can support others in their struggles. Involvement with others is much larger than just seeking or giving help. For example, joining a running or cycling club, going to evening classes, getting involved in amateur dramatics, going on group adventure holidays demonstrates your enthusiasm for pursuing new experiences and gathering more friends. This is just as important as facing adversity in building a resilient life (Reivich and Shatté, 2003).

Keep setting goals

Continually living life in the moment or being caught up in the thickets of your daily difficulties or responsibilities can give the impression that you never lift your eyes to see the horizon, i.e. where your life is headed. Goals give direction to your life, show that it has meaning and purpose, and serve as challenges to keep you on your toes. Make sure that your goals are:

- difficult (but not impossible!) to reach because the sense of goal achievement will be greater than if they're easy to attain
- within your control to achieve
- stated in clear, specific, measurable and positive terms, i.e. what you want rather than what you don't want (e.g. 'I want to pay off my mortgage within the next three years').

As Grant and Greene (2001: 77) point out: 'Goals that are both specific and difficult lead to the highest performance [and] commitment to goals is most critical when goals are specific and difficult.' Also, are your goals in alignment with your core values (those standards, principles or priorities which are of fundamental importance to you)? Paying off your mortgage is a high priority as you want to become self-employed, with all its uncertainties, in the next few years and you don't want it hanging over your head.

Persaud (2005: 38) remarks that the life worth living is goal oriented: 'All personal pride, self-esteem and self-confidence stem from the realization of difficult worthwhile goals.'

Lifelong resilience

Achieving a goal doesn't mean that you will be able to keep it (e.g. even though you've stopped smoking dozens of times, you keep returning to it). You may have struggled long and hard to overcome an adversity but, unfortunately, your hard-won resilience skills are not now set in stone. These skills need to be practised on a regular basis to avoid them atrophying. Practice can be gained through regular psychological workouts to keep you mentally sharp and setting difficult goals to pull better performances out of yourself. Maintaining resilience also includes dealing with inevitable setbacks in your progress. Setbacks can be seen as welcome learning opportunities as they help you to understand yourself better by pinpointing where your vulnerabilities still lie. Reading about resilience and talking to others about it, including eliciting from them their own stories of dealing with tough times, helps to broaden and deepen your understanding of the subject. In the final chapter, I present a summary of the key lessons for developing and maintaining resilience.

Chapter 10

An overview of resilience

Introduction

In this final chapter, I would like to pull together the material from the previous ones in order to provide an overview of resilience. When tough times threaten or appear without warning, you have choices to make such as: finding a constructive way to deal with them by experimenting with various problem-solving options; burying your head in the sand and hoping that they will disappear; looking to others to deal with them for you; or withdrawing into self-pity and helplessness by complaining continually about unwanted events in your life and believing there is nothing that you can do about them. The first choice is the resilient response, though some of the individuals I've presented in this book took the other routes before, however reluctantly, summoning up the energy and determination to face their difficulties. What follows are key lessons to remember in developing and maintaining resilience.

It's a capacity open to all to learn

This is what the research consistently confirms. It's not the special gift of an extraordinary few, but within the grasp of the ordinary many. You already have some resilience strengths or factors whether you know it or not: 'The wonderful thing about promoting resilience is that some resilience factors are almost always in a person. These can be identified and built upon and other resilience factors [which may be weak or non-existent] can be promoted at the same time' (Grotberg, 2003: 250). When I see my clients, I ask them what strengths they can call on to help them with their current difficulties. 'Strengths? I'm not sure.' You usually show determination, self-discipline and problem-solving abilities in other areas of your life, so we want to see how these qualities can be used in the current situation, as well as discovering what other strengths need to be developed in order to make further progress, for example, learning to be more tolerant of your mistakes rather than condemning yourself for making them.

See resilience as coming back rather than bouncing back from adversity

Coping with hard times (such as your house being repossessed) usually involves pain and struggle as you push forward to find a brighter future. You need time to adapt to the new realities in your life and to process your feelings about the changes and losses you've experienced as part of the self-righting process. This process of adjusting to new conditions suggests that coming back from adversity is the more realistic response. Bouncing back presents a picture of a rapid, pain-free, almost effortless return from adversity – the comic-book version of resilience. Also, if you pride yourself on being the 'bouncing back' type, you're more likely to put yourself down if your latest 'bounce' doesn't take off; for example, faced with an unfamiliar situation where your usual problem-solving skills are proving ineffective, you conclude that you're not making progress because you're weak and feel ashamed that your failings have been exposed for all to see.

Resilience is not just about dealing with adversity

You can apply the attitudes and skills of resilience to the challenges you face on a daily basis by searching for other more helpful ways of responding to, for example, traffic jams, long meetings, argumentative colleagues, late and crowded trains. In the last example, you can choose whether or not to be angry about having to stand all the way to your destination, but don't blame your anger on not getting a seat. You can't bend reality to your dictates – 'I've bought my ticket so I must have a seat!' – by conjuring up a seat for you when there isn't one to be had. Resilience also involves seeking new experiences and opportunities, in other words, taking risks. Risk taking is likely to mean some setbacks and rejections, but at least you're attempting to make more of your life rather than creeping cautiously through it trying to be certain that everything you attempt will work out in your favour.

Attitude is the heart of resilience

More precisely, sturdy but flexible attitudes will enable you to adapt to changing conditions in your life. The quickest way to discover how well or badly you are currently faring with your difficulties is to pinpoint what attitudes you hold. For example, endless 'Why did this happen to me?' speculation is turning into self-pity and making you feel helpless in the face of adverse events versus 'As this did happen to me, what do I need to start doing to regain control of my life?' which leads to constructive engagement with the situation and the feeling of empowerment in misfortune.

However, this doesn't mean that these attitudes will remain fixed: the first person may tire of self-pity and throw himself into vigorous action while the second person may falter more and more as she realizes that the road to recovery is longer than she initially thought and wonders if it's worth keeping on. So it's not as clear as it may seem at the outset of people's struggles as to who will and will not make it in the longer term. If you think that your attitude is not helping you in your struggles or has outlived its usefulness, you can change it, as the many case examples presented in this book have demonstrated. Remember, there is always more than one way of looking at events in your life. A common question I ask my clients is: 'Where are you stuck in your thinking so that it prevents you from doing what's needed to achieve your goal?'

Act in support of your resilient attitudes

Expressing resilient attitudes is easier than demonstrating them in action. If you don't act consistently and persistently in support of your new attitudes they are likely to wither away through lack of behavioural conviction in them (how many of your New Year's resolutions fizzle out a few days later through inaction?). Behaviour can be divided into action tendencies, i.e. what you may or may not do in any given situation, and completed actions, i.e. what you actually did in that situation. If your goal is to complete within a six-month period all the unpleasant tasks you've been avoiding, then you need to grit your teeth and get on with them, ticking off each task as a completed action as well as fighting against – not always successfully – the strong 'pull' of your problem-perpetuating action tendencies to avoid doing the tasks.

You can say that you're acting resiliently when your behaviour is, most of the time, completing action steps towards your goals and thereby keeping to a minimum succumbing to your action tendencies to avoid goal-directed striving. When this ratio of helpful behaviour (e.g. 85 per cent of the time) to unhelpful behaviour (15 per cent) in pursuit of your goals begins to move in the opposite direction, your self-defeating ideas (e.g. 'I can't stand doing all this hard work') are again becoming dominant in your thinking and urgent attention is required to challenge and change them.

Manage negative emotions

A resilient response to adverse events is not devoid of emotion. Expect to feel bad when bad things happen to you. Trying to put on a brave face usually means you're attempting to suppress how you really feel, which signals incomplete emotional processing of the adverse experience and then leaves you poorly prepared for the next one. For example, telling your friends that 'it's no big deal' when your girlfriend dumps you (inside you're hurt and bewildered but afraid to show it in case it's seen by them as 'being a wimp') tips over into depression when your next relationship is short lived and she goes off with one of your friends. Being resilient means being flexible, so you're not stuck in your negative feelings, they don't paralyse you. Remember that you feel as you think and changing how you think changes how you feel, thereby reducing the frequency, intensity and duration of your negative feelings. In the above example, you accept, albeit reluctantly, that you're not immune from being dumped more than once, but in looking to learn from these experiences you note that your clinginess may be offputting and seek to correct this.

Distinguish between what is within and outside of your control

It can be easy for you to fix your vision on what's outside of your control such as believing you can make your colleagues respect you. You can't make them – that's within their control – but you can change your own behaviour (e.g. improving your timekeeping, meeting deadlines, giving your honest opinions rather than manufacturing ones to please others) which might then influence them to change their opinion of you. Other examples: you can't stop yourself from getting older but you can keep yourself physically fit and mentally sharp relative to your age; you can't stop people rejecting you but you don't then have to reject yourself. Focusing on what you can't control wastes valuable time and energy that would be better spent on activities which are definitely within your control to carry out.

When adversity strikes, remembering this distinction can help you to stay in relative control of yourself as you move through the adversity: 'My thoughts, feelings and behaviours are within my control so I can choose how I want to respond to these events whereas my house being burgled and my car being vandalized are outside of my control to prevent, though I wish, of course, that these things hadn't occurred.'

Learn from whatever happens to you in life

No experience has to be wasted. What have you distilled from each situation? Here are some examples. You put yourself down when you have setbacks – such as not getting a much sought after promotion – which gives you two problems for the price of one: lack of promotion coupled with self-condemnation for not getting it; so you conclude that the least number of problems to contend with at any given time is the wisest policy to pursue. You got into a terrible temper when struggling unsuccessfully to put together a self-assembly bookcase, but decided nevertheless to persist with it unangrily in order to raise your level of frustration tolerance for carrying out boring or difficult tasks. You quickly defended yourself (not for the first time) when criticized by a colleague that, you now realize, could have helped you to improve your performance if you were prepared to listen to what he had to say – your new watchword is 'Listen first, respond later after digesting their comments'. Meaning can be found in whatever happens to you if you're prepared to search for it, perhaps in discussions with friends, rather than expect the meaning to be automatically revealed to you without any mental effort on your part.

Self-belief

In Chapter 5, I listed what I consider to be some of the strengths underpinning resilience. In this section, I want to absorb some of these strengths into this heading. Self-belief is the strong, but not unrealistic, conviction that you can move your life in the direction you want it to go. For example, in my own case, I maintained the belief that one day I would become an author through diligence and the possession of some talent. In retrospect, I realized I had served a long apprenticeship before my first book was published by being a voracious reader, studying the works of my favourite writers and practising what I considered to be good writing.

Developing self-belief means setting goals, some of increasing difficulty, and persevering until you've achieved them. Self-belief without perseverance shows you're a dreamer instead of a doer. Achieving your goals increases your confidence in your ability to do what you say you're going to do. You're not thrown into helpless despair when you encounter setbacks in your progress as they're to be expected and act as valuable learning opportunities. In fact, you don't take success or defeat too seriously.

Self-belief embraces compassionate self-acceptance as a fallible human being. You don't make any global ratings of yourself (e.g. stupid, perfect) as you realize that such ratings can never capture the complexity of you as a person, but you do label your particular behaviours in terms of whether they help or hinder you in reaching your goals (e.g. too much wine in the evenings is getting in the way of finishing your paperwork in a timely fashion). Don't turn self-belief into arrogance so that you won't admit mistakes and refuse to seek or accept help from others as you believe you have nothing to learn from them.

Maintain your resilient outlook

Having come through dark times successfully, you might believe you're now stress resistant and can rest on your laurels. Your resilience skills are likely to weaken if you don't practise them through setting challenges for yourself that take you outside of your current comfort zone (e.g. getting on with redecorating the house rather than keep putting it off because you don't feel in the mood or leaving an unsatisfying relationship rather than being stuck in it because you dread the upheaval it will cause in your life as well as the prospect of living alone). Maintaining resilience is a lifelong project to provide you with a range of attitudes and skills that you can draw on in times of misfortune.

A final word

I frequently see clients who believe that their problems are insurmountable and understandably feel pessimistic about achieving any real progress, yet several months later some of them can't believe how much change they've achieved (others remain, for example, stuck in victim mode, want near-effortless change, accept events passively as they believe they're fated to occur or wrongly think that insight alone is sufficient to promote change). How does this transformation occur for these clients? It's a willingness to be open to new ways of thinking and acting without insisting on knowing the outcome before it has occurred, persevering to reach their goals, gathering along the way resilience-promoting knowledge from both their successes and setbacks, and through their struggles seeing themselves as stronger than they previously imagined themselves to be. Because they were prepared to take the risk of changing the direction of their lives, they uncovered this inner strength which is likely to stand them in good stead for the rest of their lives. You don't really know what you're capable of achieving until you decide to put yourself to the test.

References

Antony, M. M. and Swinson, R. P. (1998) *When Perfect isn't Good Enough: Strategies for Coping with Perfectionism*. Oakland, CA: New Harbinger.

Auerbach, J. E. (2006) Cognitive coaching, in D. R. Stober and A. M. Grant (eds) *Evidence Based Coaching Handbook*. Hoboken, NJ: Wiley.

Beck, A. T. (1988) *Love Is Never Enough*. New York: Penguin.

Bonanno, G. A. (2006) Grief, trauma, and resilience, in E. K. Rynearson (ed.) *Violent Death: Resilience and Intervention Beyond the Crisis*. New York: Routledge.

Boniwell, I. (2006) *Positive Psychology in a Nutshell*. London: PWBC.

Brinkman, R. and Kirschner, R. (2002) *Dealing With People You Can't Stand*. New York: McGraw-Hill.

Brooks, R. and Goldstein, S. (2003) *The Power of Resilience: Achieving Balance, Confidence, and Personal Strength in Your Life*. New York: McGraw-Hill.

Burns, D. D. (1999) *Feeling Good: The New Mood Therapy Revised and Updated*. New York: Avon Books.

Butler, G. and Hope, T. (2007) *Manage Your Mind: The Mental Fitness Guide*, 2nd edn. Oxford: Oxford University Press.

Chartered Institute of Personnel and Development (2008) Work-related stress. Online. Available at http://www.cipd.co.uk/subjects/health/stress (accessed 10 August 2008).

Coutu, D. (2003) How resilience works, in *Harvard Business Review on Building Personal and Organizational Resilience*. Boston, MA: Harvard Business School Press.

Crowe, M. (2005) *Overcoming Relationship Problems: A Self-Help Guide Using Cognitive Behavioral Techniques*. London: Robinson.

Csikszentmihalyi, M. (1997) *Creativity: Flow and the Psychology of Discovery and Invention*. New York: Harper Perennial.

Dato, R. (2004) The mistaken notion of good stress, *Stress News*, 16 (3): 11–12.

Dryden, W. (2001) *Reason to Change: A Rational Emotive Behaviour Therapy (REBT) Workbook*. Hove, UK: Brunner-Routledge.

Dryden, W. and Gordon, J. (1994) *How to Cope When the Going Gets Tough*. London: Sheldon Press.

Dweck, C. S. (2006) *Mindset: The New Psychology of Success*. New York: Random House.

Edelman, S. (2006) *Change Your Thinking: Overcome Stress, Combat Anxiety and Improve Your Life With CBT*. London: Vermilion.

Ellis, A. (1977) *Anger: How to Live With and Without It*. Secaucus, NJ: Citadel Press.

Ellis, A. (2001) *Feeling Better, Getting Better, Staying Better: Profound Self-Help Therapy for Your Emotions*. Atascadero, CA: Impact Publishers.

Epstein, N. B. (2004) Cognitive-behavioral therapy with couples, in R. L. Leahy (ed.) *Contemporary Cognitive Therapy: Theory, Research, and Practice*. New York: Guilford Press.

Fennell, M. (1999) *Overcoming Low Self-Esteem: A Self-Help Guide Using Cognitive Behavioral Techniques*. London: Robinson.

Flach, F. (2004) *Resilience: Discovering a New Strength at Times of Stress Revised Edition*. New York: Hatherleigh Press.

Forward, S. and Frazier, D. (1997) *Emotional Blackmail*. London: Bantam Press.

Frankl, V. (1985) *Man's Search for Meaning*. New York: Washington Square Press.

Frankl, V. (1997) *Recollections: An Autobiography*. New York: Insight Books.

Gilson, M. and Freeman, A. (1999) *Overcoming Depression: A Cognitive Therapy Approach for Taming the Depression BEAST (client workbook)*. New York: Oxford University Press.

Grant, A. M. and Greene, J. (2001) *Coach Yourself: Make Real Change in Your Life*. London: Momentum Press.

Grayling, A. C. (2002) *The Meaning of Things: Applying Philosophy to Life*. London: Phoenix.

Grayling, A. C. (2005) *The Heart of Things: Applying Philosophy to the 21st Century*. London: Weidenfeld & Nicolson.

Groopman, J. (2006) *The Anatomy of Hope: How You Can Find Strength in the Face of Illness*. London: Pocket Books.

Grotberg, E. H. (1999) *How to Deal With Anything*. New York: MJF Books.

Grotberg, E. H. (2003) What is resilience? How do you promote it? How do you use it?, in E. H. Grotberg (ed.) *Resilience for Today: Gaining Strength From Adversity*. Westport, CT: Praeger.

Haidt, J. (2006) *The Happiness Hypothesis: Putting Ancient Wisdom and Philosophy to the Test of Modern Science*. London: Arrow.

Hastings, M. (2007) *Nemesis: The Battle for Japan, 1944–45*. London: Harper Perennial.

Hauck, P. (1980) *Calm Down*. London: Sheldon Press.

Hauck, P. (1981a) *Making Marriage Work*. London: Sheldon Press.

Hauck, P. (1981b) *How to Stand Up for Yourself*. London: Sheldon Press.

Hauck, P. (1991) *Hold Your Head Up High*. London: Sheldon Press.

Hauck, P. (1998) *How to Cope With People Who Drive You Crazy*. London: Sheldon Press.

Herrmann, D. (1999) *Helen Keller: A Life*. Chicago, IL: University of Chicago Press.

Hoopes, L. and Kelly, M. (2004) *Managing Change with Personal Resilience*. Raleigh, NC: MK Books.

Irvine, W. B. (2009) *A Guide to the Good Life: The Ancient Art of Stoic Joy*. New York: Oxford University Press.

Janoff-Bulman, R. (1992) *Shattered Assumptions*. New York: Free Press.

Keller, H. (1903/2007) *The Story of My Life*. Teddington: Echo Library.

Knaus, W. (2002) *The Procrastination Workbook*. Oakland, CA: New Harbinger Publications.

Kottler, J. A. (2001) *Making Changes Last*. Philadelphia, PA: Brunner-Routledge.

Leahy, R. L. (2001) *Overcoming Resistance in Cognitive Therapy*. New York: Guilford Press.

Leahy, R. L. (2006) *The Worry Cure: Stop Worrying and Start Living*. London: Piatkus Books.

Lewis, B. (2008) *Hammer and Tickle: A History of Communism Told Through Communist Jokes*. London: Weidenfeld & Nicolson.

Linley, P. A., Joseph, S., Harrington, S. and Wood, A. M. (2006) Positive psychology: past, present, and (possible) future, *Journal of Positive Psychology*, 1 (1): 3–16.

Long, G. (trans.) (2004) *Epictetus: Enchiridion*. New York: Dover Publications.

MacDonald, G. (2004) *A Resilient Life*. Nashville, TN: Nelson Books.

McKay, M. and Fanning, P. (1991) *Prisoners of Belief: Exposing and Challenging Beliefs that Control Your Life*. Oakland, CA: New Harbinger Publications.

Maddi, S. R. and Khoshaba, D. M. (2005) *Resilience at Work: How to Succeed No Matter What Life Throws at You*. New York: Amacom.

Mandela, N. (1995) *Long Walk to Freedom*. London: Abacus.

Marinoff, L. (2004) *The Big Questions: How Philosophy Can Change Your Life*. London: Bloomsbury.

Michelon, P. (2008) Brain plasticity: how learning changes your brain. Online. Available at http://www.sharpbrains.com (accessed 13 August 2008).

Morris, T. (2004) *The Stoic Art of Living: Inner Resilience and Outer Results*. Chicago, IL: Open Court Publishing.

Myers, D. G. (2004) *Intuition: Its Powers and Perils*. New Haven, CT: Yale Nota Bene.

Nay, W. R. (2004) *Taking Charge of Anger*. New York: Guilford Press.

Neenan, M. and Dryden, W. (2002a) *Cognitive Behaviour Therapy: An A–Z of Persuasive Arguments*. London: Whurr.

Neenan, M. and Dryden, W. (2002b) *Life Coaching: A Cognitive-Behavioural Approach*. Hove, UK: Brunner-Routledge.

Neenan, M. and Dryden, W. (2004) *Cognitive Therapy: 100 Key Points and Techniques*. Hove, UK: Brunner-Routledge.

Newman, R. (2003) In the wake of disaster: building the resilience initiative of APA's public education campaign, in E. H. Grotberg (ed.) *Resilience for Today: Gaining Strength From Adversity*. Westport, CT: Praeger.

Nezu, A. M., Nezu, C. M. and D'Zurilla, T. J. (2007) *Solving Life's Problems: A 5-Step Guide to Enhanced Well-Being*. New York: Springer.

O'Connell Higgins, G. (1994) *Resilient Adults: Overcoming a Cruel Past*. San Francisco, CA: Jossey-Bass.

Oyebode, F. (2007) Exercise and mental health, in R. Persaud (ed.) *The Mind: A User's Guide*. London: Bantam Press.

Padesky, C. A. (1994) Schema change processes in cognitive therapy, *Clinical Psychology and Psychotherapy*, 1 (5): 267–278.

Padesky, C. A. (2008) Uncover Strengths and Build Resilience with CBT: a 4-step model, workshop, London, 12–13 May.

Palmer, S. and Cooper, C. (2007) *How to Deal With Stress*. London: Kogan Page.

Papházy, J. E. (2003) Resilience, the fourth R: the role of schools in this promotion, in E. H. Grotberg (ed.) *Resilience for Today: Gaining Strength From Adversity*. Westport, CT: Praeger.

Pattakos, A. (2008) *Prisoners of Our Thoughts: Viktor Frankl's Principles for Discovering Meaning in Life and Work*. San Francisco, CA: Berrett-Koehler.

Persaud, R. (2001) *Staying Sane: How to Make Your Mind Work for You*. London: Bantam Press.

Persaud, R. (2005) *The Motivated Mind: How to Get What You Want From Life*. London: Bantam Press.

Redsand, A. S. (2006) *Viktor Frankl: A Life Worth Living*. New York: Clarion Books.

Reivich, K. and Shatté, A. (2003) *The Resilience Factor: 7 Keys to Finding Your Inner Strength and Overcoming Life's Hurdles*. New York: Broadway Books.

Rutter, M. (1987) Psychosocial resilience and protective mechanisms, *American Journal of Orthopsychiatry*, 57 (3): 316–331.

Sapadin, L. and Maguire, J. (1996) *It's About Time: The 6 Styles of Procrastination and How to Overcome Them*. New York: Penguin.

Sartre, J.-P. (1944/1989) *No Exit and Three Other Plays*. London: Vintage.

Seligman, M. E. P. (1991) *Learned Optimism*. New York: Knopf.

Seligman, M. E. P. (2003) *Authentic Happiness: Using the New Positive Psychology to Realize Your Potential for Lasting Fulfillment*. London: Nicholas Brealey.

Sherman, N. (2005) *Stoic Warriors: The Ancient Philosophy Behind the Military Mind*. New York: Oxford University Press.

Siebert, A. (1999) *The Survivor Personality: How to Thrive and Survive in Any Life Crisis*. London: Thorsons.

Siebert, A. (2005) *The Resiliency Advantage: Master Change, Thrive Under Pressure, and Bounce Back From Setbacks*. San Francisco, CA: Berrett-Koehler.

Stockdale, J. B. (1993) *Courage Under Fire: Testing Epictetus's Doctrines in a Laboratory of Human Behavior*. Stanford, CA: Hoover Institution Press.

Ubel, P. (2006) *You're Stronger Than You Think: Tapping into the Secrets of Emotionally Resilient People*. New York: McGraw-Hill.

Vaillant, G. E. (1993) *The Wisdom of the Ego*. Cambridge, MA: Harvard University Press.

Walen, S. R., DiGiuseppe, R. and Dryden, W. (1992) *A Practitioner's Guide to Rational-Emotive Therapy*, 2nd edn. New York: Oxford University Press.

Walsh, F. (2006) *Strengthening Family Resilience*, 2nd edn. New York: Guilford Press.

Warburton, N. (2007) *Thinking From A to Z*, 3rd edn. Abingdon: Routledge.

Warren, R. and Zgourides, G. D. (1991) *Anxiety Disorders: A Rational-Emotive Perspective*. New York: Pergamon Press.

Werner, E. and Smith, R. (1982) *Vulnerable but Invincible: A Study of Resilient Children*. New York: McGraw-Hill.

Wessler, R. A. and Wessler, R. L. (1980) *The Principles and Practice of Rational-Emotive Therapy*. San Francisco, CA: Jossey-Bass.

Wolin, S. J. and Wolin, S. (1993) *The Resilient Self: How Survivors of Troubled Families Rise Above Adversity*. New York: Villard Books.

Index